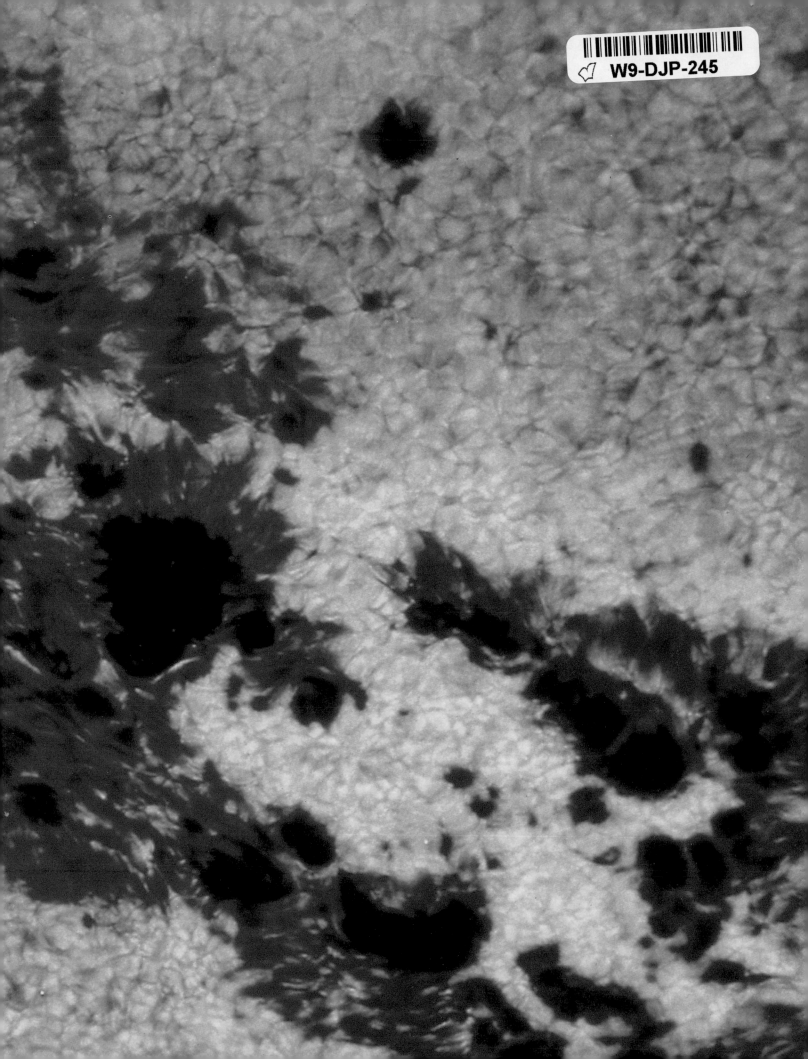

The Peter Bedrick Young People's Encyclopedia

The Universe

The Editors of Larousse

PETER BEDRICK BOOKS

NTC/Contemporary Publishing Group

Library of Congress
Cataloging-in-Publication Data

The Universe / by the editors of
Larousse ; [English translation by
Donald Gecewicz].
       p. cm. (The Peter Bedrick
young people's encyclopedia)
Originally published: France :
Larousse-Bordas, 1996.
    Includes index.
    ISBN 0-87226-624-9
    1. Astronomy—Juvenile
literature.   2. Space sciences—
Juvenile literature.   I. Larousse
(Firm)   II. Series.
QB46.U5513   2000
                    00-45516
                    CIP

This volume forms part of the Young
People's Encyclopedia. It was produced
under the editorial direction of Claude
Naudin and Marie-Lise Cuq. Text by
Philippe de La Cotardière, assisted by
Pascale Cheminée, Olivier Cornu, and
Anne Luthaud.

Graphic design and art direction by
Anne Boyer, assisted by Emmanuel
Chaspoul
Layout by Corinne Leveuf
Proofreading, revision by Annick Valade,
assisted by Isabelle Dupré, Françoise
Moulard
Picture editing by Anne-Marie Moyse-
Jaubert
Picture research by Michele Kernéïs
Production by Annie Botrel
Cover by Gérard Fritsch, assisted by
Véronique Laporte

English translation by Donald Gecewicz

First published in the United States in
2001 by Peter Bedrick Books
a division of NTC/Contemporary
Publishing Group, Inc.
4255 West Touhy Avenue, Lincolnwood
(Chicago) IL 60712-1975 U.S.A.
Copyright © 1995 by Larousse-Bordas
Translation copyright © 2001 by
NTC/Contemporary Publishing Group,
Inc.

Printed in France
International Standard Book Number:
0-87226-624-9

01 02 03 04   8 7 6 5 4 3 2 1

The Universe

The panorama of the Universe spreads out across these pages: the sun, the planets, the stars, the galaxies . . . As they probe the depths of space, astronomers are tracing our history back to the Big Bang.

How to use this book

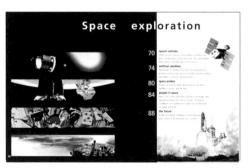

This volume is divided into four parts. Each part is introduced by an outline listing the various chapters and giving a short summary of their contents.

Double-page photograph spreads punctuate the book and allow you to discover spectacular views, such as that of an aurora borealis or of a repair carried out in space.

The appendices list important dates, statistics, and events, as well as providing biographies of famous astronomers and astronauts.

An index gives quick page references for the particular information you are looking for.

chapter title
Each chapter unfolds over one or two double-page spreads.

introductory text
At the beginning of each chapter there is a summary of the subject to be described in the following pages.

panoramic photograph
This illustrates one of the topics of the chapter.

marginal texts
These contain additional information.

The Moon is the Earth's only natural satellite. Its phases and eclipses have been observed by people for thousands of years. It is the only part of the solar system explored by astronauts.

The Moon

- **crater:** a hole made in the surface of a planet or asteroid by the impact of a meteorite.
- **full Moon:** lunar phase during which the Moon is on the opposite side from the Sun relative to the Earth and appears as a complete disk shining.
- **lunar eclipse:** disappearance (partial or total) of the Moon in the shadow of the Earth. It can only happen at full Moon.
- **lunar month:** duration of the complete cycle of the Moon's phases, about 29.5 days.
- **new Moon:** phase of the Moon during which it travels between the Earth and the Sun and cannot be seen.
- **phase:** each of the apparent shapes of the Moon in the course of its movement around the Earth.
- **quarter:** the phase of the Moon when it is seen as a half-disk. The first quarter is seen at the beginning of night, and the last quarter at the end of night.
- **solar eclipse:** partial or total disappearance of the Sun behind the Moon. It can only happen during a new Moon.

The Moon is about 384,400 km (238,862 mi) away from us. In space terms, this is not far, and the Moon looks quite large to us. In fact, with a diameter of only 3,476 km (2,160 mi), the Moon is not as wide as the continental United States.

The visible side of the Moon

Visible side, hidden side
The Moon does not produce light. It only reflects light that it receives from the Sun. The side facing the Sun is always bright, the side facing away is always dark. As the Moon rotates on its axis at the same rate as it revolves around the Earth (taking four weeks), it always shows us the same side—the visible, bright side. The other side is the hidden, dark side.

The phases of the Moon
The Moon changes position relative to the Sun, and these positions are known as **phases**. When the Moon is between the Sun and the Earth, we cannot see it. This is a **new Moon**. Two or three days later, it appears in the evening, in the west, as a thin luminous crescent. This crescent enlarges day by day. After a week, the Moon has covered a quarter of its orbit around the Earth and shows us half of its bright side. This is the first **quarter**, visible in the evening. Next it appears to be oval, the gibbous Moon. Having covered half its orbit, the Moon is on the opposite side from the Sun (relative to the Earth). Its round face shines through the night. This phase is the **full Moon**. After this, the process is reversed. The Moon again appears gibbous, then only half the lunar disk can be seen. This is the last quarter, visible in the morning. Some days later, the Moon again shows as a thin crescent. Finally, it disappears. This is the new Moon, and the

beginning of a new cycle of phases. The period between two new moons is about 29.5 days, known as a **lunar month**.

Lunar eclipses
Occasionally, during full Moon, a shadow crosses the lunar surface and blots out its light for an hour or more. This is an eclipse of the Moon, or **lunar eclipse**. The shadow passing across the Moon is that of the Earth. When the Moon is plunged into complete darkness, the eclipse is total. If only part of the Moon is in darkness, the eclipse is partial. During an eclipse of the Moon, the rounded edge of the Earth's shadow can be seen. Usually, the Moon passes just above or just below the Earth's shadow. This is why lunar eclipses do not occur at each full Moon. There can be two or three a year, sometimes none.

Solar eclipses
The Moon's diameter is 400 times smaller than the Sun's, but it is 400 times closer to Earth. This is why Moon and Sun seem the same size in the sky. When the Moon passes between the Earth and the Sun (at new Moon), the Moon may conceal the Sun for a short time. This is an eclipse of the Sun, a **solar eclipse**. When there is a total eclipse of the Sun, it becomes dark during the day and, around the black disk of the Moon, an irregular luminous halo called the solar corona is seen. While lunar eclipses can be seen from the half of the Earth where it is night, solar eclipses are visible only within a narrow band on the Earth's surface. Moreover, since the Moon revolves around us at more than 3,500 km/h (2,175 mph), solar eclipses last only a few minutes. Each year there are from two to five solar eclipses, only one of which is total.

A crescent Moon. The shadowed part can just be seen.

Stages in a total eclipse of the Sun.

Annular eclipse of the Sun
When the Moon is too far from Earth to cover the surface of the Sun completely, a narrow, bright ring remains visible at the height of the eclipse.

Solar eclipse
When the Moon travels between the Earth and the Sun, a solar eclipse happens. The eclipse can be partial, total or annular.

Lunar eclipse
At full Moon, when the Moon is at the opposite side of the Earth in relation to the sun, it is hidden by the Earth's shadow. This is a lunar eclipse.

crescent — first quarter — gibbous Moon — full Moon — gibbous Moon — gibbous quarter — crescent

26   27

---

mini dictionary
Difficult words used in the text are defined here.

heading
Each subsection expands on a basic aspect of the subject.

photo caption
This explains the illustration.

illustrations
Scientific or technical subjects are further explained by the illustrations.

c o n t

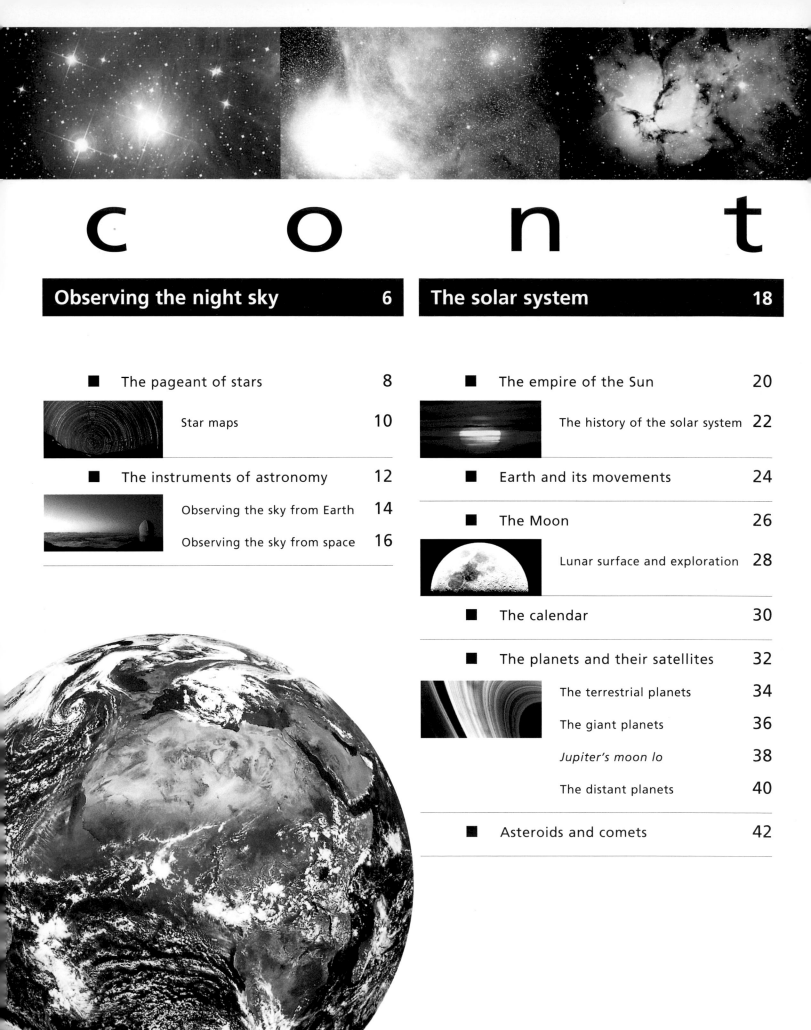

e n t s

Observing

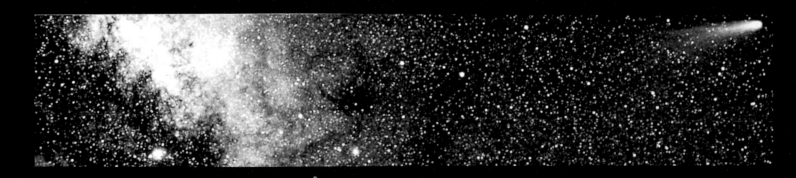

the night sky

The pageant of stars

The night sky is a magnificent spectacle for us all to see. Its appearance varies depending on the time of night, the time of year, and the point on the Earth's surface from which we observe the sky.

- ◑ **celestial body:** a natural body in the heavens such as a planet or star.
- ◑ **celestial pole:** each of two imaginary points where the axis of the Earth's poles passes through the celestial sphere.
- ◑ **celestial sphere:** immense moving sphere pictured by

early astronomers; its center is the Earth and the stars are supposedly positioned on it.
- ◑ **constellation:** a group of stars in the night sky, which form a shape or pattern, to which a name has been given; also the area of sky including this group of stars.
- ◑ **diurnal movement:** from the Latin *dies* for "day," rotational movement that the sky seems to make around the Earth in a day.
- ◑ **hemisphere:** one of the two halves of a globe, the northern and southern halves of the Earth.
- ◑ **planet:** a nonluminous (light-giving) body revolving around a star.
- ◑ **star:** a very hot body of gases, producing and giving off light.

At night, when it is not cloudy, a multitude of brilliant specks shines in the sky. Some are **planets** which, like the Earth, revolve around and are lit by the Sun. All the rest are extremely distant suns or **stars**. To appreciate the stars, you need to find a viewing site well away from city lights. With the unaided eye, you can then learn to recognize some stars, to notice differences in their brightness or color, and to follow their paths across the sky.

Stars and constellations
In the night sky, about 6,000 stars can be seen with the unaided eye. Some 20 stars are very bright. In ancient times, scientists classified the stars in **constellations** based on the shapes outlined by groups of neighboring stars. Over 2,000 years ago, the Greeks knew 48 such star groups, which they named after gods and heroes (such as Orion, Cassiopeia and Andromeda). Most constellations in the southern hemisphere were not visible from

Europe and were not named until much later, in the 1600s and 1700s. Many are named after scientific instruments (Telescopium, the Telescope) or birds (Corvus, the Crow).

The Milky Way
In both the northern and southern hemispheres, a hazy, white trail is seen hovering in the night sky, like an immense belt or sash. It is a great accumulation of stars, so many in fact that they cannot be distinguished individually, and is known as the Milky Way.

The movement of the night sky and stars
If you look at the night sky for several hours, you will notice that the stars change their positions. In the northern hemisphere, only Polaris, the pole star, stays in virtually the same place. All the others, for example, the

The movement of the stars is best seen when the night sky is photographed using a long exposure on the camera.

stars forming the Great Bear constellation, seem to revolve around the pole star. This movement becomes more evident if the night sky is photographed using a long exposure. The same phenomenon occurs in the southern hemisphere, around a point situated opposite the pole star, in the small constellation Octans. The night sky seems to rotate in a little less than 24 hours. Astronomers call this **diurnal movement**. However, this is only an apparent movement. In fact, the Earth rotates, from west to east in 23 hours 56 minutes, around an axis passing through its poles. If you observe the night sky in winter and again in summer, at the same time and from the same position, the stars will not look the same. The sky assumes an identical appearance again not in 24 hours, but in 23 hours 56 minutes—the time it takes the Earth to turn once on its axis. Therefore, if you observe the night sky at, say, eleven o'clock on one evening, you will need to look 4 minutes earlier the next evening to see the stars in the same position. After 15 days, the time difference is an hour, and over a season (three months) the difference is six hours.

The celestial sphere

To make it easier to locate the stars in the sky, people in ancient times imagined them positioned on a vast sphere, the **celestial sphere**. Its center is the Earth and it rotates around the poles, at the same rate as the planet, but in the opposite direction. In the same way as the position of a point on the Earth's surface is fixed by its latitude and longitude, the positions of the stars and planets are pinpointed by their coordinates on the celestial sphere. The spectacle offered by the night sky varies depending on your whereabouts on the Earth. Some

constellations are visible only in the northern hemisphere (for example, the Great Bear); others are seen only south of the equator (the Southern Cross).

Some stars can be seen only for a part of the night, between their rising in the east and their setting in the west, while other stars are visible all the time. Stars that revolve around the **celestial pole** are known as circumpolar stars. People who live along the equator can see the whole of the night sky pass in

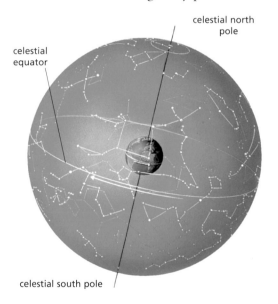

celestial north pole

celestial equator

celestial south pole

The Earth is the center of the celestial sphere, which rotates around the axis of the poles.

procession in one night. By contrast, at the North or South Pole, only half of the celestial sphere can be seen. ☐

The constellations: illusion and reality

The constellations do not exist as they are pictured. What we see are the effects of perspective. The constellation shapes are formed by stars that are in the same general direction, but at different distances from the Earth. The stars forming the Great Bear, for example, are staggered at distances ranging from 65 to about 200 light-years from us. A light-year (ly) represents the distance traveled in a year by light in a vacuum.

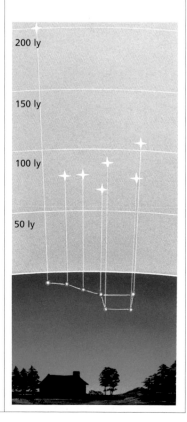

200 ly

150 ly

100 ly

50 ly

The constellation of the Great Bear

Star maps

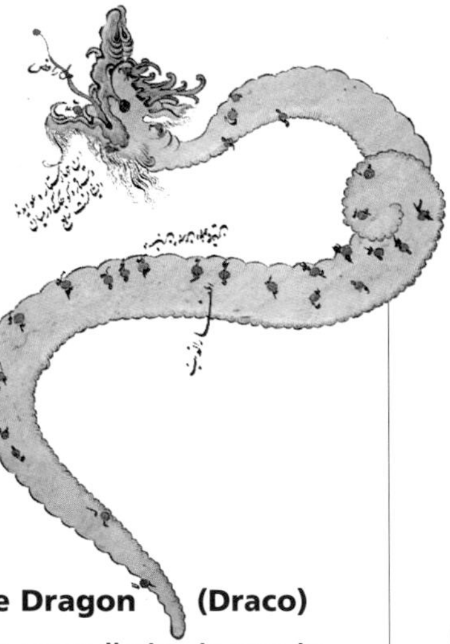

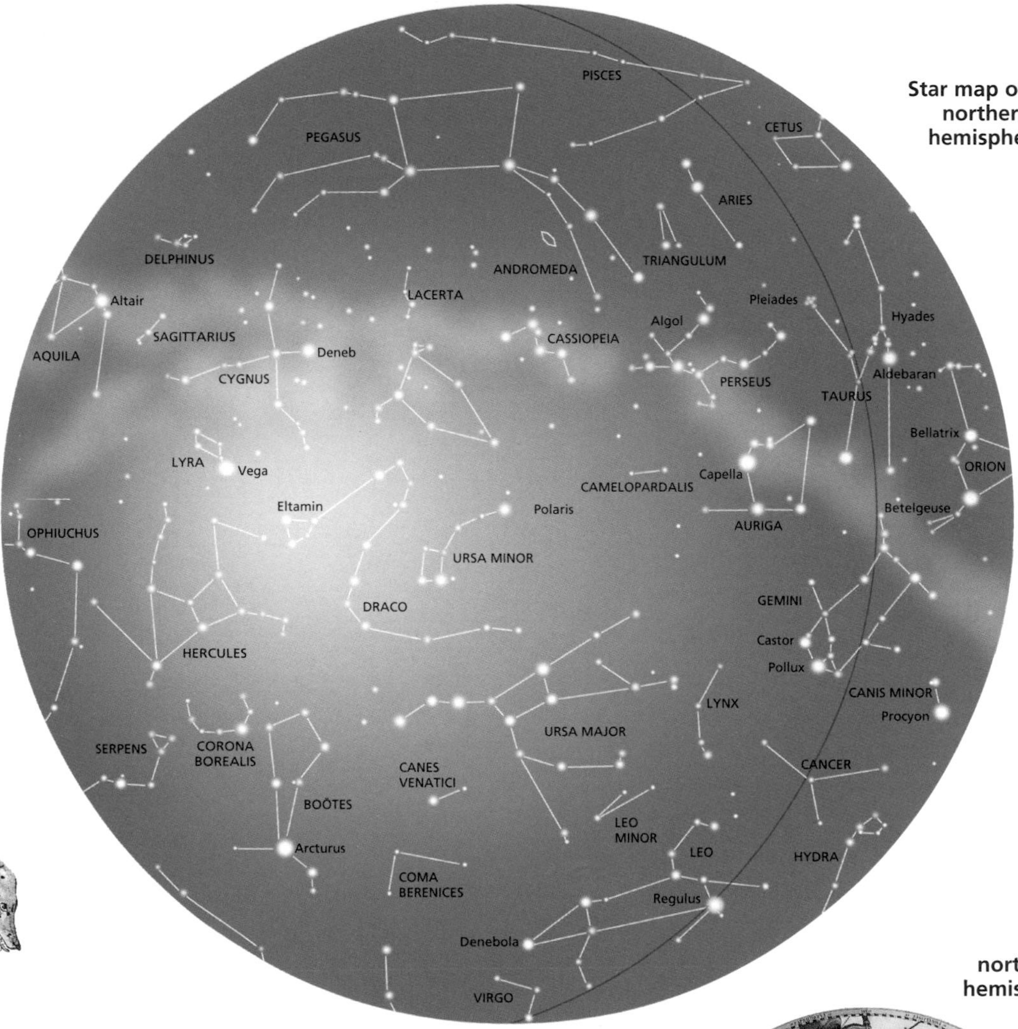

Star map of the northern hemisphere

PISCES
PEGASUS
CETUS
ARIES
TRIANGULUM
DELPHINUS
ANDROMEDA
LACERTA
Pleiades
Hyades
Altair
SAGITTARIUS
CASSIOPEIA
Algol
AQUILA
Deneb
PERSEUS
Aldebaran
CYGNUS
TAURUS
LYRA
Vega
Bellatrix
CAMELOPARDALIS
Capella
ORION
Eltamin
Polaris
Betelgeuse
OPHIUCHUS
AURIGA
URSA MINOR
GEMINI
DRACO
Castor
HERCULES
Pollux
CANIS MINOR
LYNX
Procyon
URSA MAJOR
SERPENS
CANCER
CORONA BOREALIS
CANES VENATICI
BOÖTES
LEO MINOR
HYDRA
Arcturus
LEO
COMA BERENICES
Regulus
Denebola
VIRGO

northern hemisphere

The Dragon (Draco)

This constellation is seen in the northern hemisphere. It is named after the hundred-headed monster that in Greek myth, guarded the golden apples of the Hesperides, and was slain by the Greek hero Hercules.

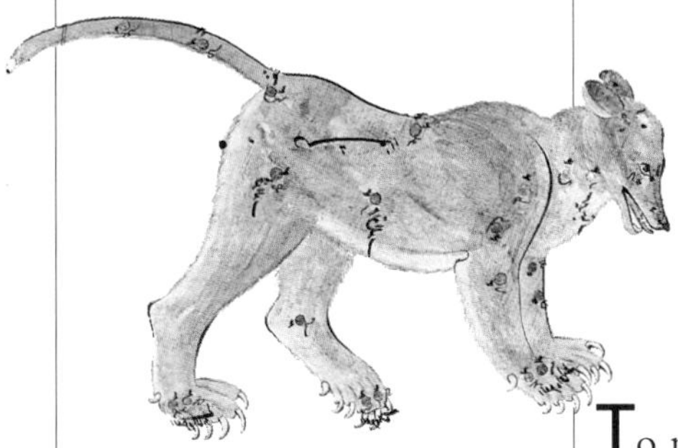

The Great Bear

The seven brightest stars of this group form the tail and body of the bear (real bears do not have long tails). To the Romans, the stars looked like a team of seven oxen. To the Arabs, they formed a coffin followed by three mourners. This constellation also contains the familiar Big Dipper.

To make it simpler for us to pinpoint individual stars, they have been grouped into 88 **constellations**. Each of these star-groups includes one group of brilliant stars that give their name to the constellation and a precise area of the night sky. The largest is Hydra and the smallest is the Southern Cross. Most constellations take their names from the myths of ancient Greece. Often you need to use your imagination to see the outline of the person, animal or object each constellation is supposed to represent.

The constellations as pictured in the 1600s

The constellation of the Southern Cross

Star map of the
southern
hemisphere

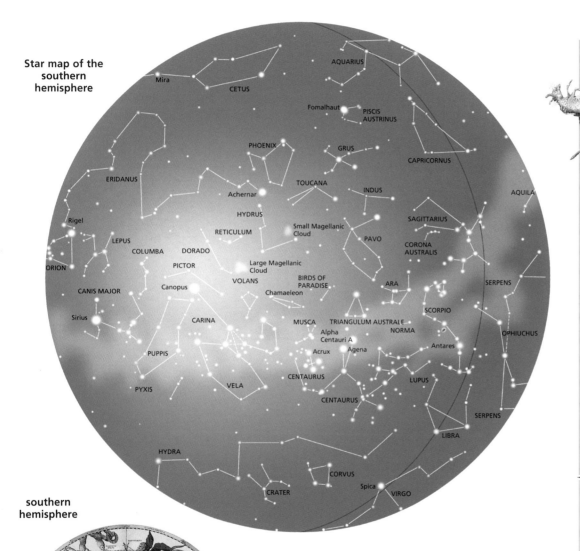

southern
hemisphere

Formerly, stars were named after their position in a constellation, the Eye of the Lion, or Orion's Shoulder, for example. Old star names such as Betelgeuse and Sirius are still used, but modern astronomers prefer to refer to stars by a letter of the Greek alphabet, followed by the abbreviation of the Latin name of the constellation to which they belong. The first letter of the Greek alphabet, α (alpha), shows the brightest star in the constellation, the second letter, β (beta), shows the second brightest, and so on. ☐

The Centaur (Centaurus)

The ancient Greeks named this constellation of the Southern Hemisphere after the centaur Chiron, a mythological creature—half-man and half-horse. It includes the star nearest to our solar system, Proxima Centauri.

The Archer (Sagittarius)

The Greeks saw this star group as the outline of a centaur about to shoot an arrow from a drawn bow. This constellation is in the Milky Way and contains a vast number of stars.

The study of the stars is called astronomy, and the scientists who specialize in this study are astronomers. They use various instruments to detect and analyze the visible light and invisible radiation from the stars.

The instruments of

atmosphere: layer of gas surrounding planets, in particular the Earth.

eyepiece: optical system in a telescope that magnifies the image presented by the objective.

objective: principal mirror of a reflecting telescope or principal lens of a refracting telescope, which collects the light from the stars.

radiation: a form of energy made up of waves or particles, moving very fast through space.

radio telescope: instrument that collects radio waves given off by the stars.

reflecting telescope: telescope in which a combination of curved mirrors collects light. Most astronomical telescopes are reflectors.

refracting telescope: simplest telescope with combinations of glass lenses to magnify distant objects, such as stars.

satellite: a body that orbits a planet, either natural (a moon) or artificial (a spacecraft).

space probe: an unmanned spacecraft designed to explore the planets and asteroids of the solar system.

spectrum: pattern obtained when radiation is broken into its various parts. When ordinary sunlight passes through a glass prism, it breaks or disperses into a rainbow-colored band.

The first astronomers observed the heavens with the naked eye. In the 1600s, two optical instruments were invented to improve on the power of the human eye, the **refracting telescope** and the **reflecting telescope**. The first person to use a refracting telescope to look into space was an Italian, Galileo Galilei (1564–1642). In 1671, the British scientist Isaac Newton (1642–1727) made the first reflecting telescope. Today, astronomers do not often observe stars directly. Instead, they use computers to sharpen and analyze the images that telescopes provide.

Photographing the stars
Photography has been used by astronomers since the late 1800s. A photographic plate of film gradually accumulates the light it receives, so several hours of exposure can produce a photograph of very faint stars invisible to the human eye. However, a plate or film records only a small proportion of the light shining onto it. So now astronomers use electronic equipment that is far more light-sensitive. The picture is displayed on a television screen that may be near the telescope or thousands of kilometers away.

Radiation from the stars
The human eye and telescopes are both sensitive to light. But the stars also emit other forms of radiation, which are invisible, such as radio waves, infrared and ultraviolet rays, x rays and gamma rays. The coldest stars mainly give off infrared rays. The hottest stars are powerful sources of x rays and ultraviolet rays. Special telescopes can pick up these rays. Radio waves are received on Earth by **radio telescopes**. The other types of radiation are filtered out by the Earth's **atmosphere**. To study them, instruments must be sent into space on board **satellites**. The Moon and the

planets orbiting the Sun are close enough to us to be studied directly by space probes.

Analyzing light from the stars
Robot space probes have given us close looks at some planets. But for the stars, everything we know comes from studying the light and invisible radiation we receive from them. Astronomers have tried to perfect instruments to analyze light. The spectroscope, for example, is used to study the light given off by stars or reflected from planets. When light

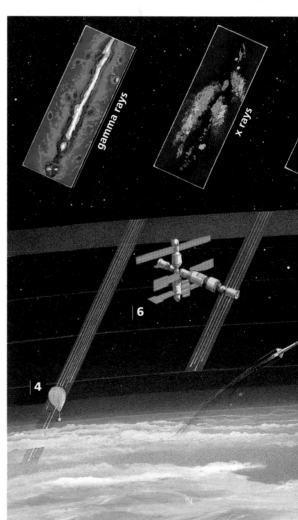

The M31 Galaxy in Andromeda

astronomy

passes through a spectroscope, it is broken up into a rainbow–colored band marked with alternate light and dark lines. This is known as the **spectrum** of the star. Another instrument, the spectrograph, is used to photograph a star's spectrum directly. The photometer measures the intensity of light from a star, which indicates its temperature. ☐

Studying light and radiation
Optical telescopes (1) collect visible light from stars. To study invisible radiation (such as radio waves, x rays, infrared and ultraviolet rays), other instruments are used including: radio telescopes (2) on the ground; in the atmosphere, aircraft (3), balloons (4) and sounding-rockets (5); and in space, satellites and space telescopes (6, 7, 8). ■

Three views of Andromeda
The pictures below show Andromeda observed by three kinds of instruments.

In visible light (top), through a telescope, the galaxy's spiral shape is seen, with billions of stars whirling around a bright center.

Infrared telescopes reveal those areas richest in dust.

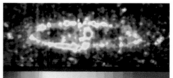

Radio waves, as seen by a radio telescope, detect the presence of gases among the stars. Although more than 2 million light-years distant, Andromeda is one of our closest neighbor-galaxies, and one of the best known.

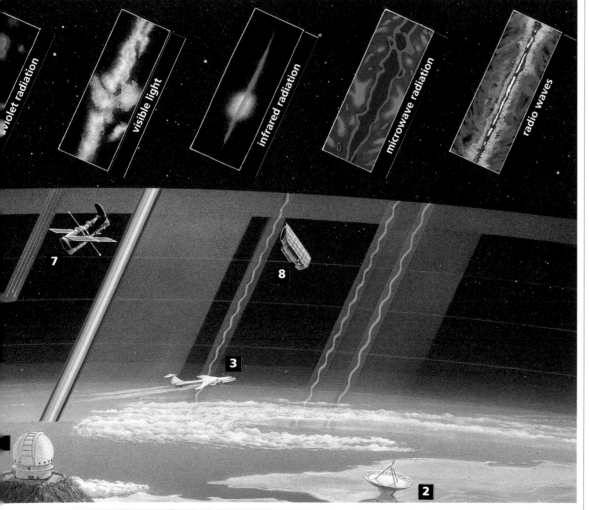

The Mauna Kea observatory in Hawaii, above the clouds

Observing the sky from Earth

sun visor
objective
tube
eyepiece

A small refracting telescope

The objective inside the tube is made up of a lens, or series of lenses. The light from the stars passes through the lens and is magnified by the eyepiece. The image is seen by simply looking through the eyepiece.

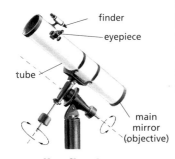

finder
eyepiece
tube
main mirror (objective)

A small reflecting telescope

Here the objective is a curved mirror that reflects the light. The light rays converge on a second mirror to form an image. A small refracting telescope, known as the finder, is fixed to the body of the telescope to make it easier to aim the instrument at the target star.

To collect light from the stars, astronomers use two main types of instruments: the refracting telescope and the reflecting telescope. Stars also give off radio waves, and these invisible signals can be picked up on the ground by radio telescopes.

Refracting and reflecting telescopes

Both kinds of telescope are basically a tube containing an optical system, known as the **objective**, which is pointed toward the sky. This device collects light from the stars at which it is aimed and gives an image of them. The two telescope types have different objectives. The refracting telescope has a glass lens, while the reflecting telescope has a mirror that reflects the incoming rays of light. By looking through a kind of magnifying glass, the **eyepiece**, the scientist can see the image directly. The image can also be photographed or recorded and analyzed using electronic equipment.

Different mountings

Telescopes must be movable, so they can be pointed toward different parts of the sky. Reflecting and refracting telescopes are fitted to mountings which allow them to move both round and round, and up and down. Big telescopes have motors to do this. In the equatorial mounting, the telescope's axes of

The Keck 1 telescope in Hawaii is the world's biggest refracting telescope.

movement are aligned with the Earth's poles and equator, so that it can remain aimed on a particular target star for as long as is necessary, as if the Earth were not spinning on its own axis. In the altazimuth mounting, the telescope revolves around horizontal and vertical axes. This simple arrangement is used with small telescopes (as shown by the arrows in the diagrams, left). It is also used in large telescopes that have a computer to keep the instrument fixed on the star to be observed.

Giant telescopes

The performance of a telescope depends on the size of its objective—the bigger the objective, the better the instrument. The larger the surface area of the objective, the more light it receives, enabling it to detect radiation from very faint objects, such as distant stars. A large-diameter objective

The VLA radio telescope in Socorro, New Mexico

enables two luminous points that are close together to be more easily separated and shows greater detail. Astronomers now use telescopes with very large mirrors. These are installed on mountain tops, such as the peak of Mauna Kea in Hawaii, where the air is clearer and better for observation.

Radio telescopes

Radio astronomy is the study of radio waves given off by the stars. These waves are picked up on the ground by **radio telescopes**. They do not have mirrors but instead have much bigger metal dishes, usually from 10 to 25 m (33 to 82 ft) in diameter. The flow of radio waves from a star can be so faint that they are amplified before being recorded and analyzed. The most effective instruments are those with the biggest collecting surface. Building radio telescopes with dishes as big as fields is hardly practical, but equally good results can be obtained from a number of smaller dishes spaced out. An example is the VLA (Very Large Array) telescopes in Socorro, New Mexico. Radio dishes in different countries, or even different continents, can be linked. They do not operate all at once. Instead the signals they detect are recorded on tape and then mixed. This is know as Very Long Baseline Interferometry.

What starlight can tell us

When light from a star passes through a glass prism, it breaks up into a band in the colors of the rainbow, known as the spectrum. Usually, this colored band is crossed by dark lines. These lines indicate which chemical elements have absorbed part of the light on its journey from the star. A star's spectrum gives information not just about its chemical composition but also about its temperature and movement in relation to the Earth.

The mirror of the Keck 1 telescope measures 10 meters (33 feet) across.

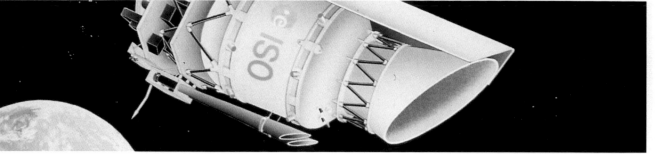

The ISO satellite

Observing the sky from space

Sounding rocket

Observations from these rockets last no more than a few minutes before the rocket falls back to Earth. The instruments and scientific data are recovered by parachute.

Balloon

Before bursting, a balloon can carry an instrument package for several weeks.

The Kuiper Airborne Observatory

This is a C-141 aircraft converted by NASA into a flying observatory. It flies 12,000 m (39,000 ft) high, studying sources of infrared radiation in space. In 1977, it discovered the rings around the planet Uranus.

Some types of radiation from stars do not reach the Earth's surface. They are filtered out by the **atmosphere**. Telescopes to study these rays can be sent up high into the atmosphere, by plane, balloon or rocket, and into space, aboard satellites. Instruments on **space probes** launched toward our neighbor planets can make other observations.

Aircraft, balloons and rockets

An aircraft can fly high enough to get above most of the atmosphere, especially the cloud cover. Clouds are laden with water vapor, which absorbs infrared radiation from stars. Balloons can reach heights of 40 km (25 mi). They are used to study stars giving off gamma rays or infrared rays. Sounding rockets fired several hundred kilometers above the Earth detect x rays and ultraviolet radiation from the stars.

Space observatories

For longer observation above the atmosphere, telescopes are put on satellites launched into orbit around the Earth. They can detect all types of radiation from the stars and can go on working for several years. Since the 1960s, astronomers have put many satellites into space. The most advanced are space observatories, controlled from the ground. Astronomers point them toward the stars they wish to study as easily as if they were on the ground. For the different types of radiation, different telescopes are used. Telescopes studying infrared rays must be cooled to a very low temperature. Those studying ultraviolet rays like the International Ultraviolet Explorer

(IUE) need a mirror made of quartz, rather than glass, while instruments collecting x rays or gamma rays are designed to detect atomic particles.

IUE satellite

The Hubble Space Telescope

The Hubble is the biggest optical telescope so far launched into space. Built jointly by the United States and Europe, it was put into orbit in 1990 by the U.S. Space Shuttle at an altitude of 600 km (373 mi). It is 12 m (43 ft) long, weights 11 tons, and has a mirror 2.4 m (8 ft) in diameter. After it was launched, images from the Hubble turned out blurred because its huge mirror was not correctly cut—it was two-thousandths of a millimeter off! This fault restricted the telescope's performance because its images had to be "enhanced" (improved) by long and expensive computer processing. Fortunately, the telescope had been designed so it that it could be repaired. In December 1993 Shuttle astronauts recovered the telescope in space and repaired it on board their spacecraft. It was fitted with a corrective device (much as a nearsighted person is fitted with eyeglasses). It was given new solar panels to produce the electrical power to drive it and a new wide–angle camera. Since then, astronomers have received photographs of distant galaxies that are far better than any taken from Earth.

Space probes

Space probes can add further information about planets. Some of these probes, such as the U.S. Voyagers, simply fly past the target planet and make only a rapid scan with their instruments. Other probes enter an orbit

The American space probe Voyager 2 passing Saturn

around the planet and so can make more detailed observations. This is how the U.S. Lunar Orbiter probes studied the Moon. The Venera probes sent to the planet Venus by the Russians actually landed on the surface, as did the U.S. Viking probes on Mars. □

The Compton satellite

Compton is NASA's second largest space observatory, after the Hubble Space Telescope. It weighs almost 16 tons, about a third heavier than Hubble. When launched, it was the largest civilian satellite. Fitted with four powerful gamma-ray detectors, it observes the most violent events in the universe and the stars that emit the most intense energy. The picture shows Compton being released into orbit from the shuttle Atlantis on 7 April

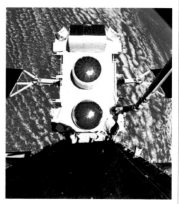

1991. The release took place 450 km (280 mi) above the Earth. First known as GRO (Gamma Ray Observatory), the satellite was renamed in orbit after the American physicist Arthur Compton.

The Hubble Space Telescope is released from the Space Shuttle and placed in orbit on 25 April 1990.

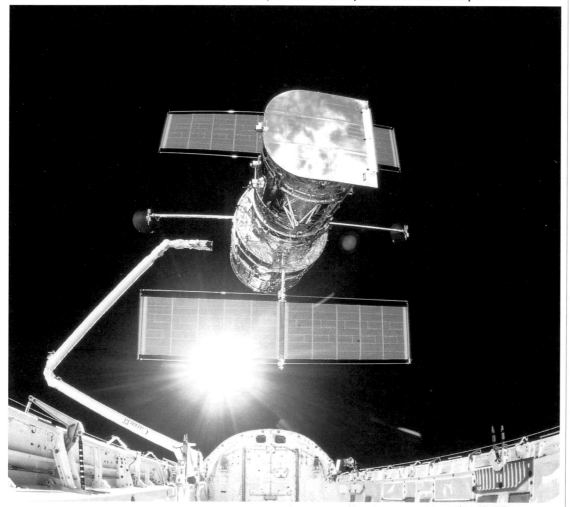

The sola

system

For us on Earth, the Sun is the most important of all the stars. It is the closest star to us. It forms, with its planets and other bodies, the solar system, of which the Earth is but a small part.

The empire of the Sun

O **asteroid:** small planet no bigger than a few hundred kilometers across.

O **comet:** small body of rock and ice that releases large amounts of gas and dust and becomes luminous as it nears the Sun.

O **meteorite:** solid body that originates in interplanetary space and may fall onto the surface planet.

O **orbit:** closed, curved path that one body moves along in space around another body (such as a star) of greater mass.

O **planet:** a celestial body that orbits the Sun and reflects light from it.

O **satellite:** body that orbits a planet, such as a moon.

O **solar system:** the Sun's family of planets, and their satellites, as well as comets, asteroids and meteorites.

O **star:** very hot, gaseous body producing and giving off light.

O **Sun:** the star around which the Earth and other planets of the solar system orbit.

O **white dwarf:** small star, very dense and faint, that represents the last stage in the evolution of a star.

The part of the universe where the Earth travels depends on the Sun. For this reason, we call it the solar (sun's) system. The system includes planets, comets, meteorites and dust.

Planets and asteroids

The main celestial bodies of the Sun's "empire" are those that, like the Earth, orbit around the Sun and reflect its light—the **planets**. There are nine major planets: Mercury (nearest the Sun), then Venus, Earth, Mars, Jupiter, Saturn, Uranus, Neptune, and Pluto. Five planets can be seen in the sky with the naked eye: Mercury,

Venus, Mars, Jupiter, and Saturn. These have been know since ancient times. As well as the nine major planets, there are many small planets or **asteroids**, concentrated mainly between the orbits of Mars and Jupiter. The biggest asteroid, Ceres, is about 1,000 km (621 mi) across. The smallest is no more than a few hundred meters in diameter. The Sun exercises a powerful gravitational attraction on all its planets, since it is almost a thousand times heavier than all the planets combined.

Satellites, comets, and meteorites

The largest planets have **satellites** moving around them. In the case of the Earth, there

Neptune

Earth

Sun

Mars

Mercury

Venus

Jupiter

is one satellite, the Moon. The solar system also includes **comets**, small bodies formed of rocks and ice which, when they approach the Sun, release great quantities of gas and dust. Collisions between asteroids and the breakup of comets that come too close to the sun or the larger planets produce debris of varying sizes. This debris circulates in interplanetary space, before finally falling onto the planets or their satellites in the form of **meteorites**.

The vastness of the solar system

The planets are distributed around the Sun in the form of a disk. This disk has a radius of about 6 billion km (3.7 billion mi). Sunlight takes about six hours to cross it. Although the solar system seems enormous, compared to the universe as a whole, it is minute. Imagine the Sun reduced to the size of an orange. On this scale, the planet Pluto would be no bigger than a pin head circling the orange at a distance of 400 m (1,300 ft) away. The nearest star to the Sun would be 3,000 km (1,900 mi) away from the orange! ☐

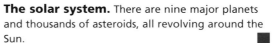

The solar system. There are nine major planets and thousands of asteroids, all revolving around the Sun. ■

The Sun viewed from the Earth

At a distance of about 150,000,000 km (93,000,000 mi) from our planet, the Sun appears to us as a dazzling disk in the sky. Its light takes eight minutes to reach us and blots out all other starlight. The effect of the Sun's rays passing through the Earth's atmosphere gives the sky its blue color.

The Sun viewed from Pluto

Pluto is about 40 times farther away from the Sun than is the Earth. From Pluto, the Sun would look no bigger than one brilliant star in a dark sky.

Pluto

Saturn

Uranus

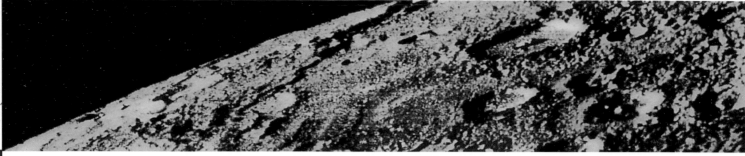

The surface of Mercury

The history of the solar system

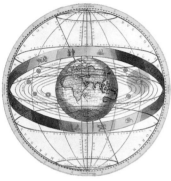

Ptolemy's universe

For centuries, people believed that the Earth was the center of the universe and that the Sun and planets revolved around it. This world system was described by the Greek scientist Ptolemy in the 2nd century AD.

By studying the planets and stars, astronomers can reconstruct the history of the solar system and predict its possible future.

The formation of the solar system

The Sun was formed from an immense cloud of gas and dust. For reasons still not fully understood, perhaps as a result of the explosion of a large nearby star, this cloud began to collapse under its own weight and to turn in on itself. Gradually, it took the form of a disk, denser and hotter in its center than at its edges. In the center of the disk, matter became dense and hot enough for the Sun to begin to shine. This happened about 4.6 billion years ago. In the immense cloud of gas and dust, solid particles were squashed together to form the planets, which took less than a hundred million years. Near the Sun, where the heat was greatest, planets were formed from rocky chunks. In this way, Mercury, Venus, Earth and Mars were shaped. In the colder, outer regions, rocks and ice merged to form the cores of huge planets. These cores attracted large quantities of gas from the original cloud of matter. This is how Jupiter, Saturn, Uranus and Neptune were formed.

The future of the solar system

The solar system is destined to disappear.

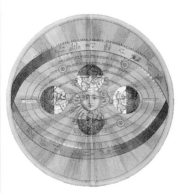

The Copernican universe

In the 1500s, the Polish astronomer Copernicus claimed that the Earth and planets in fact revolved around the Sun. After the invention of the refracting telescope in the 1600s, he was proven right.

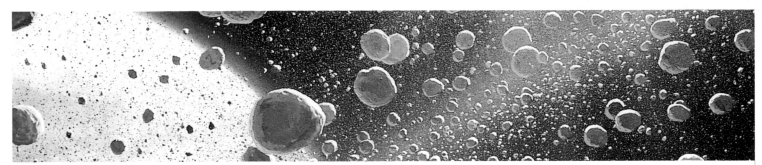

From the moment the Sun began to shine, its energy (light and heat) has come from nuclear reactions that transform hydrogen into the slightly heavier gas, helium. In fewer than 5 billion years, all the hydrogen in the Sun's center will have disappeared. The Sun will begin to swell up and change into a giant red star, a red giant. The Earth will then begin to burn up: its surface temperature will soar to around 2000°C, enough to melt rocks into molten lava. Long before that, the oceans will have dried up and all life will be gone. In its final stage of life, the Sun will stop swelling. Its matter will contract to form a small star the size of the Earth but immensely more dense. This **white dwarf** will quietly fade away, plunging the solar system into cold and darkness. ☐

Birth, life and death of the solar system.

The solar system was born 4.6 billion years ago from a cloud of gas and dust (1) that rotated and flattened into a disk (2). At the center of the disk, the Sun began to shine (3), and the planets were formed (4). In 5 billion years, the Sun will evolve into a red giant (5, 6, 7) before shrinking into a white dwarf that will slowly burn out. ■

Other solar systems?

In 1984, astronomers discovered an immense disk of dust surrounding the star Beta Pictoris.

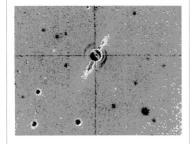

In the picture above, the disk (colored yellow by computer) is seen side on. Detected through infrared observations, it is probably a young solar system. Astronomers believe that many stars may have one or more planets circling them. Our present instruments cannot easily detect such planets directly. To see from Earth a planet the size of Jupiter orbiting one of the closest stars would be as hard as seeing from Paris a candle 10 m (33 ft) away from a powerful lighthouse in New York! Nevertheless, in 1992, astronomers confirmed the presence of two planets circling a star 1,600 light-years away from Earth.

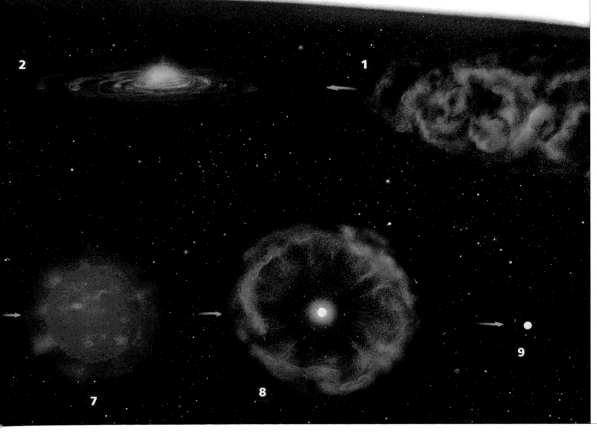

The Earth rotates on its own axis, and it also moves around the Sun. These two movements give us day and night, and the cycle of the seasons, which regulate life on Earth.

Earth and its move-

The Earth is the third planet from the Sun, after Mercury and Venus. It is not perfectly round but a sphere that is slightly swollen at the equator and flattened at the poles. Its radius is 6,378 km (3,963 mi) at the equator and 6,357 km (3,950 mi) at the poles. Water covers 71 percent of the Earth. Around the planet is a layer of gases, the **atmosphere**, formed of air, a compound based on nitrogen and oxygen.

The revolution of the Earth

Like all planets in the solar system, the Earth revolves around the Sun. When the Earth has completed one full circuit, or **revolution**, a **year** (roughly equivalent to 365.25 days) has passed. The average distance of the Earth from the Sun is about 149.6 million kilometers (93 million miles). Astronomers use the astronomical unit (a.u.) to refer to this distance, and they often use this unit instead of kilometers or miles to express distances between the planets of the solar system. The distance between the Earth and Sun varies during the year, from a minimum of 147.1 million kilometers (91.4 million miles) at the **perihelion** (around 3 January) to a maximum of 152.1 million kilometers (94.6 million miles) at the **aphelion** (around 6 July). The average speed at which the Earth travels around the Sun is roughly 108,000 km/h (67,000 mph). This speed increases when the planet approaches the Sun and decreases as it moves away from it.

The Earth's rotation

At the same time as it moves around the Sun, the Earth spins on its axis. Its axis of **rotation**, known as its "polar axis," is an imaginary line through the planet between the north and south poles. The axis of rotation is at an angle of 66°34′ to the Earth's plane of orbit. The rotation on its own axis causes the alternation of day and night, because the two halves or hemispheres of the Earth do not face the Sun at the same time. This explains

The Earth viewed from space

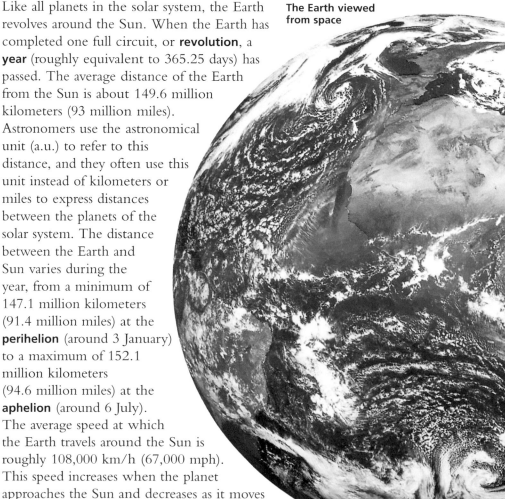

ments

why we see the Sun rise, climb in the sky, descend below the horizon and set. It is not the Sun that moves, but the Earth in relation to the Sun. Measured in relation to the stars, the Earth's rotation on its axis takes 23 hours 56 minutes and 4 seconds. This is the sidereal day. Measured in relation to the apparent movement of the Sun, the solar day, the rotation takes about 4 minutes longer. For convenience, we take each day to be 24 hours exactly.

Seasons, equinoxes and solstices

If the Earth rotated about its axis perpendicularly (to the plane of its orbit) the Sun would shine on it in the same way all year, and there would be no seasons. The tilt of the axis of rotation gives the northern and southern hemispheres different exposures to the Sun's rays at different times of the year.

In its movement around the Sun, the Earth passes through four positions that mark the seasons in temperate regions on Earth. We call these the equinoxes and solstices. During the **equinoxes** (20 or 21 March and 22 or 23 September), the line separating the half of the Earth lit by the Sun from the half in darkness passes through the poles. At all latitudes (regardless of distance from the equator), the hours of daylight are identical, and night and day are equal length. During the **solstices** (21 or 22 June and 22 or 23 December), the line separating the half of the Earth lit by the Sun from the half in darkness passes through the polar circle (latitude 66°34' north or south of the equator) and forms its greater angle relative to the poles. The discrepancy

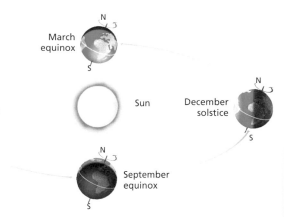

Revolution and rotation of the Earth

The Earth revolves around the Sun and also rotates about its own inclined axis through the poles. The combined effects of these two movements produce the seasons.

between day and night is then at its greatest. The Sun lights one of the poles, and in that half of the Earth days are at their longest. The other pole is in darkness, and in its half of the Earth, nights are at their longest. The March equinox marks the beginning of spring in the northern hemisphere and of autumn in the southern hemisphere. The December solstice marks the beginning of winter in the northern hemisphere and of summer in the southern hemisphere.

Precession

The polar axis revolves, like the axis of a spinning top, in just under 26,000 years. This movement is known as precession, and explains why the "pole star" has not always been the same star.

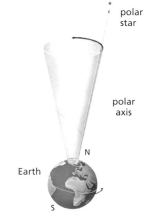

Movement toward the apex

The Sun is moving at 72,000 km/h (45,000 mph) through space toward the apex, a point situated in the constellation Hercules. This causes the planets orbiting the Sun, including the Earth, to move in a spiral.

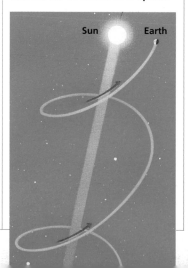

The Moon

The Moon is the Earth's only natural satellite. Its phases and eclipses have been observed by people for thousands of years. It is the only part of the solar system explored by astronauts.

The visible side of the Moon

The Moon is about 384,400 km (238,862 mi) away from us. In space terms, this is not far, and the Moon looks quite large to us. In fact, with a diameter of only 3,476 km (2,160 mi), the Moon is not as wide as the continental United States.

Visible side, hidden side

The Moon does not produce light. It only reflects light that it receives from the Sun. The side facing the Sun is always bright, the side facing away is always dark. As the Moon rotates on its axis at the same rate as it revolves around the Earth (taking four weeks), it always shows us the same side—the visible, bright side. The other side is the hidden, dark side.

The phases of the Moon

The Moon changes position relative to the Sun, and these positions are known as **phases**. When the Moon is between the Sun and the Earth, we cannot see it. This is a **new Moon**. Two or three days later, it appears in the evening, in the west, as a thin luminous crescent. This crescent enlarges day by day. After a week, the Moon has covered a quarter of its orbit around the Earth and shows us half of its bright side. This is the first **quarter**, visible in the evening. Next it appears to be oval, the gibbous Moon. Having covered half its orbit, the Moon is on the opposite side from the Sun (relative to the Earth). Its round face shines through the night. This phase is the **full Moon**. After this, the process is reversed. The Moon again appears gibbous, then only half the lunar disk can be seen. This is the last quarter, visible in the morning. Some days later, the Moon again shows as a thin crescent. Finally, it disappears. This is the new Moon, and the

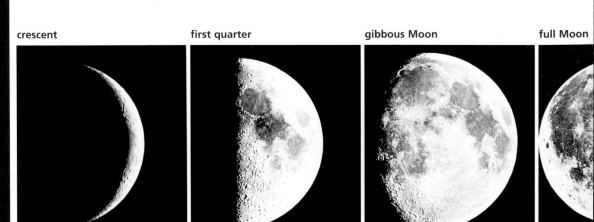

crescent   first quarter   gibbous Moon   full Moon

A crescent Moon. The shadowed part can just be seen.

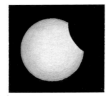

Stages in a total eclipse of the Sun.

beginning of a new cycle of phases. The period between two new moons is about 29.5 days, known as a **lunar month**.

Lunar eclipses

Occasionally, during full Moon, a shadow crosses the lunar surface and blots out its light for an hour or more. This is an eclipse of the Moon, or **lunar eclipse**. The shadow passing across the Moon is that of the Earth. When the Moon is plunged into complete darkness, the eclipse is total. If only part of the Moon is in darkness, the eclipse is partial. During an eclipse of the Moon, the rounded edge of the Earth's shadow can be seen. Usually, the Moon passes just above or just below the Earth's shadow. This is why lunar eclipses do not occur at each full Moon. There can be two or three a year, sometimes none.

Solar eclipses

The Moon's diameter is 400 times smaller than the Sun's, but it is 400 times closer to Earth. This is why Moon and Sun seem the same size in the sky. When the Moon passes between the Earth and the Sun (at new Moon), the Moon may conceal the Sun for a short time. This is an eclipse of the Sun, a **solar eclipse**. When there is a total eclipse of the Sun, it becomes dark during the day and, around the black disk of the Moon, an irregular luminous halo called the solar corona is seen. While lunar eclipses can be seen from the half of the Earth where it is night, solar eclipses are visible only within a narrow band on the Earth's surface. Moreover, since the Moon revolves around us at more than 3,500 km/h (2,175 mph), solar eclipses last only a few minutes. Each year there are from two to five solar eclipses, only one of which is total.

Annular eclipse of the Sun

When the Moon is too far from Earth to cover the surface of the Sun completely, a narrow, bright ring remains visible at the height of the eclipse.

Earth   Moon

Moon's shadow   Sun

Solar eclipse

When the Moon travels between the Earth and the Sun, a solar eclipse happens. The eclipse can be partial, total or annular.

Earth's shadow

Moon   Earth   Sun

Lunar eclipse

At full Moon, when the Moon is at the opposite side of the Earth in relation to the sun, it is hidden by the Earth's shadow. This is a lunar eclipse.

gibbous Moon   gibbous quarter   crescent

Lunar mountains

Lunar surface and exploration

Tintin on the Moon

The cartoonist Hergé drew his characters walking on the Moon 15 years before the first astronauts landed there.

Driving on the Moon

During the final Apollo missions, astronauts drove about the Moon in buggies.

If you look at the Moon through binoculars, you can see the mountains, plains and craters on its surface. However, it was not until probes and astronauts explored the Moon that its relief became known in detail.

The lunar surface

The dark patches that form the features on the face of the full Moon (when seen with the unaided eye) are plains. In former times, people thought that these plains were seas and gave them poetic names such as the Sea of Serenity, Sea of Tranquility and the Lake of Dreams. The names have been kept, even though we now know that there is no water on the Moon. The highest mountains rise to 8,200 m (26,900 ft), just a little lower than Mount Everest, even though the Moon is much smaller than the Earth.

The Moon is covered with craters of all sizes. These have been carved out by the **meteorites** that for thousands of millions of years have rained down on the Moon's surface. The largest are more than 200 km (124 mi) across. Around some craters, white ridges radiate like the spokes of a wheel. These are formed by soil debris thrown out in all directions at the time of the meteorite's impact.

Exploration of the Moon

Since 1959, many probes have been launched toward the Moon. The first probes were intended simply to photograph its surface as they passed over it or before crashing into it. In October 1959, the Soviet probe Luna 3 sent back the first pictures of the hidden side of the Moon. Probes then made soft landings

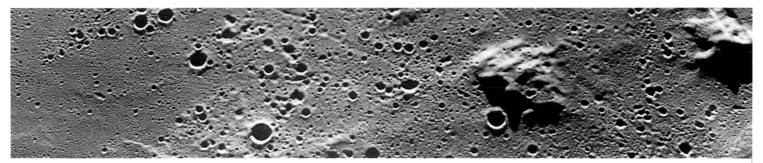

The hidden side of the Moon, photographed by the Galileo probe

and supplied more precise information about the Moon's surface. Next, satellites put into orbit around the Moon studied and photographed it over several months. Finally, people set foot on the Moon. The first two astronauts landed there on 20 July 1969. They were Neil Armstrong and Edwin Aldrin of the U.S. Apollo 11 mission. Between 1969 and 1972, 12 U.S. astronauts from six Apollo missions walked on the Moon. The Apollo astronauts took thousands of photographs of the Moon, set up scientific instruments on its surface, took various readings and brought back nearly 400 kg (892 lbs) of lunar rocks for analysis.

The surface of the Moon

Although so close, the Moon is a very different world from our own. It has no water or any trace of life. The lunar surface is strewn with stones and rocks embedded at varying depths in a thick layer of gray dust.

Humans cannot survive there without life support equipment because, unlike the Earth, the Moon has no atmosphere. The gravity on its surface is one-sixth of that on the Earth, too weak to hold down a layer of gases around it. Without an atmosphere to protect it, the Moon receives the full force of meteorites and radiation coming from space. It is directly exposed to the rays of the Sun. During the day, the temperature on the Moon's surface exceeds 100°C (212°F). At night, it can fall below –170°C (–338°F). Day and night are also much longer than on Earth: each lasts about two weeks, because the Moon takes four weeks to rotate on its axis. The sky visible from the Moon is always black, even when the Sun shines. It would be the same on Earth if there were no atmosphere, but the atmosphere diffuses the Sun's light. □

An astronaut's footprint on the lunar surface

The lunar mountains

The mountains of the Moon were discovered in the 17th century, after the invention of the refracting telescope. Most of the Moon's mountains were named after mountain ranges on Earth, such as the Alps, Apennines, Carpathians and Caucasus. From the length of their shadows on the Moon's surface, it has been possible to work out their various heights. The tallest peaks are

near the south pole of the Moon.

Before spacecraft came close to the Moon, it was thought that its mountains bristled with jagged, pointed peaks. The illustration above shows an artist's impression of such lunar mountains. Exploration has shown that Moon mountains are actually more like the Earth's older mountain ranges, with smooth faces and rounded summits.

The calendar

Since ancient times, people have felt the need of a system for ordering events in the past, present, and future. So they created calendars, which divide time into days, months, and years.

○ **calendar:** system to measure time, based on the movement of the Earth around the Sun and/or the movement of the Moon around the Earth.

○ **day:** time taken by the Earth to rotate on its own axis. This time may be measured according to different markers, such as the distant stars (sidereal day) or the Sun (solar day). In everyday life, the day is divided into 24 hours.

○ **leap year:** a year that includes an extra day in February, and thus 366 days in total.

○ **lunar month:** duration of the complete cycle of the phases of the Moon (about 29.5 days).

○ **month:** calendar division roughly the length of a cycle of the phases of the Moon.

○ **phases of the Moon:** each of the apparent shapes of the Moon in the course of its movement around the Earth.

○ **revolution:** movement of a planet around the Sun, or of a satellite around its planet.

○ **year:** time taken by the Earth (and, in a wider sense, by the other planets) to make a revolution of the Sun.

Three natural events can be used to measure time: the change between day and night, the **phases of the Moon**, and the cycle of the seasons. So, from ancient times, three natural units of time have been recognized: the **day**, linked to the Earth's rotation on its axis; the **month**, associated with the Moon's movement around the Earth; and the **year**, observed from the movement of the Earth around the Sun.

Formal systems invented to divide time into days, months and years are known as **calendars**. There are three major types: solar calendars, lunar calendars and lunisolar calendars.

Solar calendars

Solar calendars are based on the time the Earth takes to complete one **revolution** around the Sun. The year is made up of 365 days, distributed among 12 months. Periodically an extra day has to be added to account for the fact that the Earth's journey around the Sun lasts not 365 days exactly, but 365 days 5 hours 48 minutes and 46 seconds (about 365¼ days). In pre-Columbian America, the Mayas and Aztecs used a solar calendar that included 18 months each of 20 days and 5 additional days.

Aztec calendar: at the center is the Sun

The Gregorian calendar

The calendar used around the world today is a solar calendar. It was revised in 1582 by Pope Gregory XIII and is called the Gregorian calendar. Normally made up of 365 days, it is divided into 12 months: January (31 days), February (28 days), March (31 days), April (30 days), May (31 days), June (30 days), July (31 days), August (31 days), September (30

Fragment of an Aztec calendar

days), October (31 days), November (30 days) and December (31 days).

As the Earth completes its revolution around the sun in 365¼ days, every four years it is necessary to add an extra day to February. That year then has 366 days and is called a **leap year**. Years ending in 00 are only leap years if the result of their division by 400 is a whole number: the year 2000 was a leap year, but the year 1900 was not.

Ancient Egyptian calendar

Lunar calendars

Lunar calendars depend on the cycle of the phases of the Moon, known as a **lunar month**. The year is made up of twelve lunar months. Twelve lunar months have 29 and 30 days alternately, so the year only has a total of 354 or 355 days. Each year, then, the months fall 11 days short and are out of rhythm with the seasons. In three years, the calendar differs from the seasons by a month. The Muslim calendar is a lunar calendar. Each year it falls out of step from 10 to 12 days in relation to the Gregorian calendar. The ancient Egyptians used a lunar calendar with 365 days and only three seasons: akhet (flood), peret (winter) and shemou (the summer drought).

Lunisolar calendars

These are calendars combining the two methods described above. The year has 365 days, as in a solar calendar, but the months are adapted as closely as possible to the cycle of the phases of the Moon. In the Jewish calendar, the months are lunar (29 and 30 days) and the years are solar. Because 12 lunar months add up to only 354 days, it is sometimes necessary to include a complete thirteenth month to make up the difference. The traditional calendars of East Asia are also lunisolar calendars. ☐

Fragment of a Gregorian calendar:
this type of calendar is used worldwide.

The starting dates of calendars

The starting dates of different calendars vary from one civilization to another. Most peoples count years from a religious or legendary event that they regard as fundamental.

In the Muslim calendar (above), the years are counted

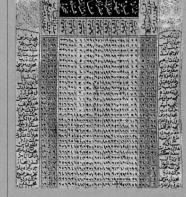

from 16 July 622, the date of the flight of the prophet Mohammed to Medina (an event known as the Hegira). In the Jewish calendar, the years are counted from a date thought to be the creation of the world: 3761 BC. The Gregorian calendar is reckoned from the year of the birth of Christ as established in the sixth century by a Scythian monk, Dionysius Exiguus. This is known as the Christian era.

The planets and their

Nine major planets and their satellites inhabit the solar system. The planets closest to the Sun are similar to the Earth. The more distant planets are different both in their volume and their composition.

○ **atmosphere:** layer of gas that surrounds some planets, in particular, the Earth.

○ **core:** central part of a planet, where its matter is heaviest per unit of volume.

○ **crust:** solid surface on planets of the Earth's type.

○ **mantle:** part of a planet of the Earth's type, located between the crust and the core.

○ **orbit:** the closed curved path that one body describes in space, around another body of greater mass.

○ **planet:** a celestial body that orbits the Sun and reflects light from it.

○ **revolution:** movement of a planet around the Sun, or of a satellite around its planet.

○ **ring:** an almost circular band made up of a mass of small solid objects (frozen rocky masses, dust) that can be observed around the largest planets of the solar system.

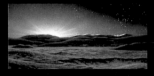

○ **rotation:** movement of a planet or asteroid around its polar axis.

○ **satellite:** a body that revolves around a planet.

The nine major **planets** of the solar system move clockwise around the Sun at distances ranging between a minimum of 45.9 million km (28.5 million mi) for Mercury, and a maximum of 7.4 billion km (4.6 billion mi) in the case of Pluto. The terrestrial planets are those closest to the Sun. The giant planets orbit at a greater distance, and farther beyond these are the distant planets.

The terrestrial planets

Mercury, Venus, Earth and Mars, the four planets closest to the Sun, are the terrestrial planets. They are formed of a quite dense rocky material, and their surface—known as the **crust**— is solid. The smallest (Mercury) has a diameter of 4,900 km (about 3,000 mi) while the largest (Earth) has a diameter of almost 13,000 km (almost 8,000 mi). These planets have changed a great deal since their formation. They have lost their initial layer of light gases and now have **atmospheres** formed from gases derived from within themselves. Their surface features, too, have changed with the course of time.

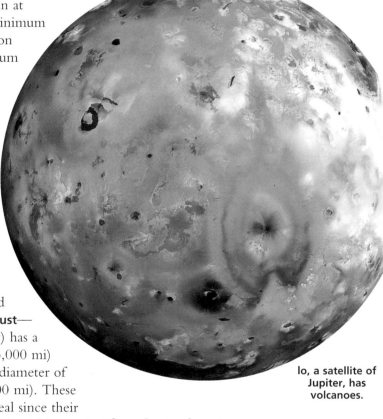

Io, a satellite of Jupiter, has volcanoes.

The giant planets

Orbiting beyond Mars are Jupiter and Saturn. They are giants, much larger than the terrestrial planets. Jupiter's diameter is about 11 times that of the Earth, Saturn's is nine times greater. However, their density is a lot less. The giants are basically spheres of gas. While they do not have solid surfaces, they do have central **cores** of

Europa is an ice-covered satellite of Jupiter.

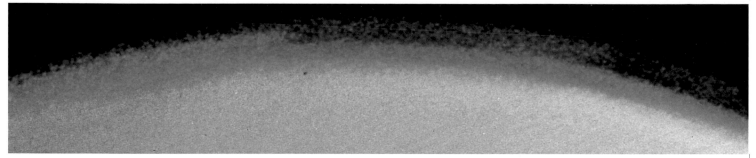

satellites

rock and ice. They have evolved very little since their formation and have conserved their original thick atmosphere based on hydrogen and helium (two light gases). They rotate very rapidly (in only 10 to 16 hours) and are surrounded by **rings** of matter.

The distant planets

Beyond Jupiter and Saturn are the three planets farthest from the Sun: Uranus, Neptune and Pluto. Uranus and Neptune are smaller than Jupiter and are basically made up of light gases, surrounded by rings. It is thought that their insides are made up of a vast mass of ice. Pluto, the most distant planet, is an oddity. It is like the terrestrial planets because of its small size but more like the larger planets in its density.

Natural satellites

Apart from Mercury and Venus, the planets of the solar system all have one or more satellites. In total, 61 satellites are now known, 27 of them discovered from photographs taken by space probes. Satellites can be classed in three families, based on their size. The largest are the Moon, Jupiter's four chief satellites (Io, Europa, Ganymede and Callisto), Saturn's largest satellite, Titan, and Neptune's major satellite, Triton. These are all more than 3,000 km (1,800 mi) in diameter. Some, such as the Moon and Callisto, are formed of rocks and others of a mixture of ice and rocks. The average-sized satellites have a diameter

of between roughly 200 and 1,600 km (120 to 1,000 mi). These satellites orbit Saturn, Uranus, Neptune and Pluto, and most are a mixture of ice and rock. Miniature satellites make up the third family. These are irregularly shaped and under 200 km (125 mi) across, the smallest being just a few kilometers in diameter. Mars has the two best know miniature satellites, Phobos and Deimos.

Jupiter's satellite Callisto is covered in craters.

The planet Jupiter

Jupiter deservedly qualifies as a giant planet. Jupiter could hold 1,300 planets the size of the Earth! In this illustration, artificial colors distinguish the various cloud layers at different altitudes.

33

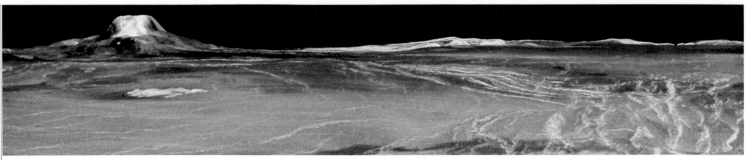

A view of the surface of Venus

The terrestrial planets

Structure of the terrestrial planets

The four terrestrial planets are formed of a light solid crust covering a heavier rocky mantle that in turn envelops a metallic core.

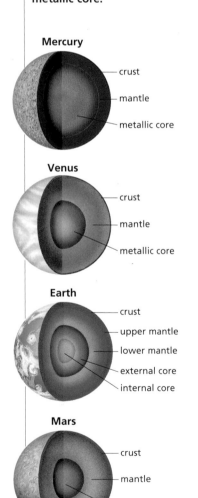

Mercury
- crust
- mantle
- metallic core

Venus
- crust
- mantle
- metallic core

Earth
- crust
- upper mantle
- lower mantle
- external core
- internal core

Mars
- crust
- mantle
- metallic core

Mercury is thought to have the heaviest core in relation to its total volume and Mars the lightest.

The surface of Mercury is covered with craters.

Although at first sight very different, the four terrestrial planets of Mercury, Venus, Earth and Mars are similar in size and structure. Since the beginning of the 1960s, space probes have been sent out to survey Venus and Mars.

Mercury

Mercury is 58 million km (36 million mi) from the Sun and takes 88 days to complete its orbit. Because it is close to the Sun and rotates on its axis slowly (in 58.6 days), its days are very hot (up to 400°C/ 752°F) and its nights very cold. It is the smallest of the terrestrial planets, at 4,880 km (3,032 mi) in diameter.

Mercury has practically no **atmosphere**, for like the Moon, it is not heavy enough to retain an envelope of gas around it. Its lack of atmosphere has meant that over thousands of millions of years it has suffered the full force of meteorites and other bodies hitting it. Mercury has no known satellite.

Venus

Venus is situated 108 million km (67 million mi) from the Sun and makes one orbit in 225 days. Its **rotation** on its axis is very slow, lasting 243 days, and is from east to west, in the opposite direction of the other planets' rotation. With a diameter of 12,100 km (7,518 mi), Venus is a little smaller than the Earth. However, Venus's atmosphere is very different. Its basic constituents are carbon dioxide (96 percent) and nitrogen (3.5 percent). It is enveloped in a thick veil of clouds divided into three layers between the altitudes of 50 and 70 km (30 and 45 mi). Some of these cause rains of corrosive sulphuric acid.

On Venus it is very hot. Under the effect of the Sun's rays, the carbon dioxide in its atmosphere acts like the glass of a greenhouse and the ground temperature can reach 460°C (860°F). The surface of Venus is covered in volcanic plains. Many of the volcanoes are apparently still active. Like Mercury, Venus has no satellite.

Earth

The Earth is about 150 million km (93 million mi) from the Sun. Its revolution takes 365.25 days, and its rotation lasts 23 hours 56 minutes. It is the largest of the four terrestrial planets, with a diameter of just over 12,700 km (7,900 mi). The Earth is enveloped by air, a mixture of gases containing nearly 78 percent nitrogen and 21 percent oxygen. The Earth is unique in

A Venera probe over Venus

being the only planet on which water is known to remain liquid, thus favoring the emergence and evolution of life. Water gradually wears away the rocks and so is partly responsible for the changing relief of the Earth's surface. The highest temperature recorded on the Earth is 58°C (136°F) in Libya, and the lowest, -89.2°C (-128.6°F) in Antarctica. The Earth has a single satellite, the Moon.

Mars

Mars is about 228 million km (142 million mi) from the Sun. It takes 687 days to make a complete revolution of the Sun and rotates on its axis in 24 hours 37 minutes. Its diameter of 6,800 km (4,225 mi) is slightly more than half of the Earth's. Since gravity on Mars is weak (about a third of the Earth's gravitational force), it can retain only a thin atmospheric layer. This is

made up of 95.3 percent carbon dioxide, 2.7 percent nitrogen, 1.6 percent argon and traces of oxygen. Farther from the Sun than the Earth, Mars is a colder planet: the ground temperature often drops to -80°C (-112°F) and never exceeds 20°C (68°F). Like Venus, Mars has traces of volcanic activity. The solar system's largest volcanoes (now extinct) are on Mars, rising to over 25 km (16 mi). The rocky, desert surface of Mars looks red. Its rocks contain an iron oxide that gives them their color, just like rust. At times, clouds of dust are raised by violent storms. Two small satellites, Phobos and Deimos, orbit Mars. ☐

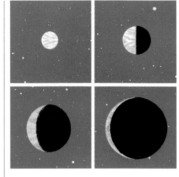

The phases of Venus

Seen from the Earth, Venus has phases, like the Moon. Venus' crescent has finer points than that of the Moon, and the apparent diameter of the planet varies greatly according to the phase. This is because its distance from the Earth varies from 41 to 258 million km (25 to 160 million miles).

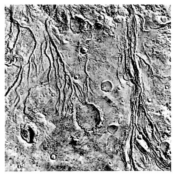

The "canals" of Mars

Some scientists think that long ago the climate of Mars was less harsh. Water may have flowed across the planet. This would explain the many winding valleys that can be seen and that resemble dried-up river beds.

A huge canyon gashed across the surface of Mars

Io and Europa passing Jupiter

The giant planets

Structure of the giant planets

These planets are basically made up of hydrogen and helium. Under the gaseous atmosphere is a layer of highly compressed hydrogen surrounding a rocky core.

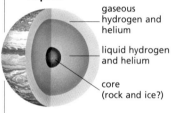

Jupiter
- gaseous hydrogen and helium
- liquid hydrogen and helium
- core (rock and ice?)

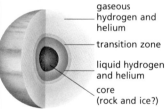

Saturn
- gaseous hydrogen and helium
- transition zone
- liquid hydrogen and helium
- core (rock and ice?)

Jupiter's red spot

The Great Red Spot has varied in size and color over time. It now covers an area 30,000 km (18,600 mi) long and 13,000 km (8,000 mi) wide. It is a gigantic hurricane within Jupiter.

Beyond Mars orbit two giant planets: Jupiter and Saturn. They are visible to the unaided eye and were observed by people in ancient times. Detailed information about them was provided by the U.S. Voyager probes, which flew by the planets between 1979 and 1981. Unlike the Earth, Jupiter and Saturn have no solid surface. They are enormous spheres.

Jupiter

Jupiter is the largest of all the planets. It has a diameter 11 times that of the Earth, a mass 318 times greater and is more than 1,300 times the Earth's volume. It is 778 million kilometers (483 million miles) from the Sun. This giant is enveloped in a thick atmosphere, based on hydrogen and helium, in which clouds circulate made up of other solidified or liquefied gases, principally methane and ammonia. Because Jupiter rotates on its axis very quickly (in less than 10 hours), these clouds stretch out in bands parallel to the equator, like belts girdling the planet. The topmost clouds appear to shine, while the other layers remain shrouded in gloom. The cloudy formations are turbulent: enormous whirlwinds are common and spring up relatively quickly. An immense red spot has long intrigued astronomers. This is a permanent hurricane, four times as big as the Earth. The top of the clouds is very cold (-148°C or -234°F), but inside the planet the temperature and pressure increase. In Jupiter's core, the temperature probably reaches 25,000°C (17,000°F) and the pressure is 50 million times that on the Earth's surface.

Jupiter, the largest planet in the solar system

Jupiter has 16 known moons. Four are large, comparable to the Moon: Io, Europa, Ganymede and Callisto. The others are small satellites, only a few tens of kilometers in diameter.

Saturn

Saturn is 9.5 times bigger than the Earth in diameter, has 95 times its mass, and is more than 750 times its volume. On average, it is 1.4 billion km (870 million mi) from the Sun. Like Jupiter, it is a gaseous sphere that rotates very quickly on its axis (in a little more than 10 hours). It is less dense than Jupiter because it has an even greater hydrogen content. On water, Saturn would float!

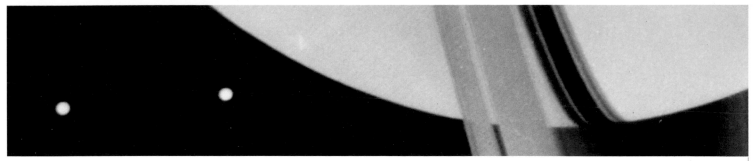

Saturn and two of its satellites

The clouds enveloping the planet are stirred by very violent movements, like cyclones. The temperature at the top of the clouds is -180°C (-292°F). Like Jupiter, Saturn has a source of internal heat. It gives off a little less than three times the amount of energy it receives from the Sun. Eighteen moons have been discovered around Saturn, including a giant, Titan, that is bigger than the planet Mercury.

The rings of Saturn

Saturn's unique feature is its visible system of rings. This ring system is so huge that it can be seen from Earth even with a small refracting telescope. Galileo glimpsed the rings around 1610, but it was the Dutch scientist Christian Huygens who in 1659 was the first to understand the phenomenon. From the Earth, only half a dozen rings could be seen, but photographs taken by the Voyager probes showed that there are thousands. They form around Saturn, on the plane of its equator, an immense disk nearly 300,000 km (186,000 mi) in diameter—but scarcely 1 km (0.6 mi) in thickness. Depending on the position of Saturn in relation to the Earth and the Sun, we see the rings as more or less inclined. Sideways, they look so thin that they cannot be seen. The rings are made up of small blocks of frozen dust that whirl around the planet like tiny satellites.

The rings of Jupiter

Jupiter's rings are a lot less spectacular than Saturn's rings. The outer edge of the main ring is 57,000 km (35,000 mi) above the highest clouds of the atmosphere. It is 6,000 km (3,700 mi) wide and extends toward the planet as a diffuse halo and in the opposite direction as a wide external ring. □

The rings of Jupiter

Jupiter has thin rings of matter that are completely invisible from the Earth. They were discovered by the Voyager space probes.

How were the rings of Saturn formed?

This is still not known for certain. Perhaps they are the debris resulting from the formation of Saturn, or the remnants of satellites that broke up because they orbited too close to the planet.

Saturn and its rings

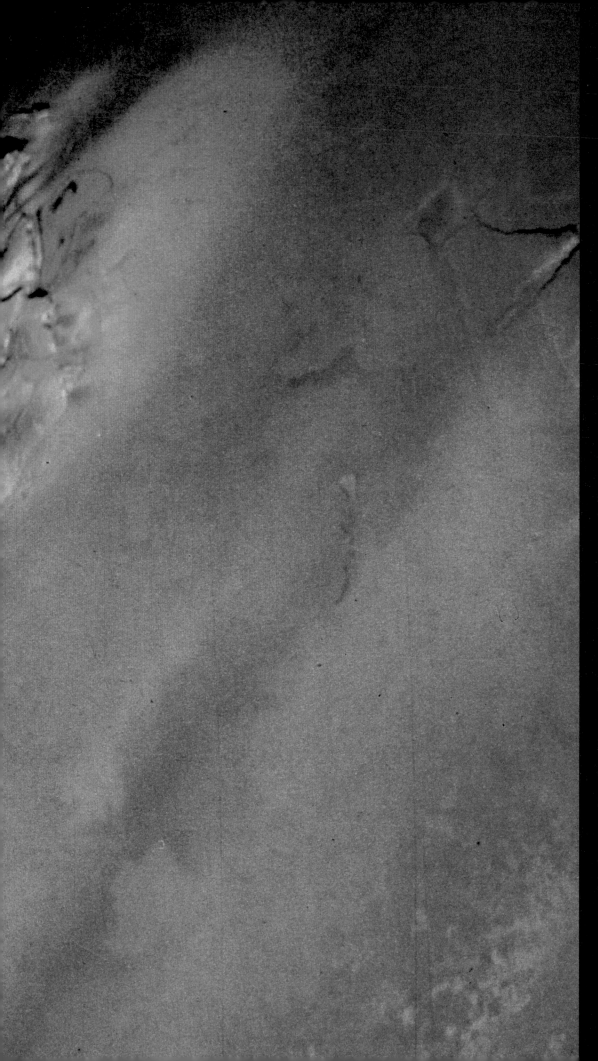

Jupiter's Moon Io

The Voyager probes produced a surprise when they revealed that the frozen surface of Io, one of Jupiter's four largest moons, has a great number of active volcanoes. Io is pulled one way by the gravitational force of the giant planet Jupiter and in the opposite direction by the planet's three other large satellites: Europa, Ganymede, and Callisto. This tug-of-war deforms and heats the matter inside Io. Periodically, matter shoots to the surface through volcanoes, like Pele, which can be seen in this photograph. Sulfurous lava is blasted out at more that 3,000 km/h (1,860 mph), and at times reaches a height of 200 km (125 mi).

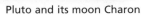

Pluto and its moon Charon

The distant planets

Beyond the giant planets are two other large planets: Uranus and Neptune. Their distance makes them difficult to study from the Earth, but they have become better known since the U.S. space probe Voyager 2 flew past Uranus in 1986 and Neptune in 1989. Pluto has never been approached by a space probe and is still something of a mystery.

Uranus

Uranus was first spotted, through a telescope, by the British astronomer William Herschel in 1781. In what was a chance sighting, he at first took it for a comet. Uranus has about 4 times the diameter of Earth and about 15 times its mass. It is 2.8 billion kilometers (1.7 billion miles) from the Sun. Although smaller and denser than Jupiter and Saturn, like those two planets it is surrounded by a thick **atmosphere**, based on hydrogen and helium. However, its atmosphere also contains methane, which gives it a beautiful blue color.

Uranus is an icebox, with a temperature that drops below –200°C (–328°F). It is thought to have a large rocky **core** covered by a thick **mantle** of of ice and is surrounded by 10 **rings** of dark dust ranging between 42,000 km (26,000 mi) and 51,00 km (32,000 mi) from the center of the planet. Fifteen satellites have been recorded around Uranus. The five largest were observed from the Earth and the others were discovered by the Voyager 2 probe.

The planet Uranus

The Earth is not the only blue planet. Uranus (above) and Neptune (at right) share this color. However, the reasons for it are different. Uranus and Neptune have atmospheres containing methane, the main constituent of natural gas used on Earth for heating. The gas absorbs the red band radiation in sunlight reaching these two planets but lets the blue band radiation pass through.

The rings of Uranus

Neptune

Neptune was discovered in 1846 in the very spot where the French astronomer, Urbain Le Verrier, had calculated that it must be. Only Neptune's presence could explain certain irregularities in the movement of Uranus. Neptune orbits at an average distance of 4.5 billion km (2.8 billion mi) from the Sun. In appearance and size, Neptune is Uranus's double. However, its atmosphere is more turbulent. Clouds propelled by winds of more than 1,000 km/h (600 mph) are visible at various altitudes. The most spectacular formation is a huge dark spot as wide as the Earth. It is rather like Jupiter's Great Red Spot, an enormous hurricane swirling at more than 600 km/h (400 mph). Small clear clouds circulate very rapidly at higher altitudes, probably formed by crystals of frozen methane.

Due to its great distance from the Sun, Neptune receives 900 times less solar energy than the Earth. However, it gives off 2.7 times as much energy as it receives. The source of this internal heat energy is not known, but it explains the planet's violent atmospheric disturbances. The Voyager 2 probe identified four rings around Neptune,

Charon as it would be seen from Pluto

The principal rings of Neptune

Neptune photographed by the Voyager 2 probe in August 1989

hidden in a disk of dust. The outer ring is unique in having three pronounced arcs along which the accumulated matter concentrates. Neptune has eight known satellites. The largest, Triton, is the coldest body known in the solar system, with a surface temperature of -228°C (-378°F).

Pluto

When it was discovered in 1930, Pluto was the most distant planet in the solar system. However, because its orbit forms an elongated ellipse, its distance from the sun varies between 4.4 and 7.4 billion km (2.7 and 4.6 billion mi). In 1979 Pluto came closer to the Sun than Neptune and remained so until March 1999. With a diameter of less than 2,500 km (1,500 mi), Pluto is smaller than the Moon. From Earth its size is equivalent to that of a coin seen at a distance of a dozen kilometers! No probe has yet reached Pluto, and very little is known about it. It is thought to be formed of a rocky **core** covered by a mantle of ice. Its surface is probably covered by frozen nitrogen and methane, and it may have a thin atmosphere containing methane. Some astronomers think that Pluto is a former satellite of Neptune that broke away as a result of a collision with another body. In 1978 Pluto was found to have a satellite, Charon, which has a diameter of about 1,200 km (750 mi), about half Pluto's. There are no other examples in the solar system of satellites proportionally as big compared with their mother planet.

Structure of the distant planets

Uranus

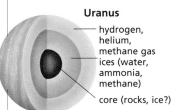

hydrogen, helium, methane gas
ices (water, ammonia, methane)
core (rocks, ice?)

Neptune

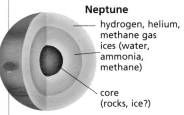

hydrogen, helium, methane gas
ices (water, ammonia, methane)
core (rocks, ice?)

Pluto

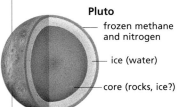

frozen methane and nitrogen
ice (water)
core (rocks, ice?)

Uranus and Neptune are formed mainly of hydrogen and helium. Pluto is a world of rocks and ice discovered using the orbital calculations of the American astronomer Percival Lowell (1855–1916).

Along with the larger planets and their satellites, thousands of smaller bodies revolve around the Sun—asteroids no larger than a hundred miles long, comets, meteorites and dust.

Asteroids and

Gaspra, the first asteroid to be flown past by a space probe.

The space between the major planets is not empty. Within it move a multitude of smaller bodies, including smaller planets known as **asteroids**. There are also **comets**, which when passing the Sun occasionally become visible to the naked eye, as well as rocky masses and dust. All this matter joined together would make a planet much smaller than the Earth.

Asteroids

Asteroids are small rocky bodies. The largest, Ceres, is less than 1,000 km (621 mi) in diameter. The smallest have irregular shapes. Astronomers think that asteroids are small "lumps" of the **nebula** from which the solar system emerged. These lumps were unable to accumulate to form a **planet** because of the powerful gravitational force exercised by Jupiter.

Over 5,000 asteroids have already been classified, and more are discovered each year. The greatest concentration of asteroids is between the **orbits** of Mars and Jupiter, at distances ranging between 320 and 495 million km (200 to 308 million mi) from the Sun. Some asteroids orbit at a much greater distance, beyond Neptune and Pluto. Others have very elongated orbits that skim past the Earth. In 1937, Hermes, a boulder less than 1,000 m (2,300 ft) across, passed our planet at a distance of 780,000 km (490,000 mi)—

twice as far away as the Moon.

The U.S. **space probe** Galileo, launched toward Jupiter, was the first to take detailed photographs of asteroids. In 1993, it sent pictures of Gaspra, measuring 19 km by 12 km (12 by 7 mi) and of Ida, measuring 52 km by 30 km (84 by 48 mi). The surfaces of both asteroids are pockmarked by craters hollowed out by the impact of **meteorites**. A miniature moon only 1.5 km (0.9 mi) across was discovered orbiting Ida.

Comets

Comets have a nucleus only a few kilometers across, a mixture of ice, chunks of rock and dust. When a comet nears the Sun, the

comets

nucleus is heated up and gives out gases and dust. It then becomes surrounded by a bright halo known as the coma. The coma trails away from the Sun as a thin, straight, bluish stream of gas, and a thicker, curved, yellow tail of dust. The tails are sometimes several million kilometers long. Most comets gradually lose their gas but conserve their rocky nucleus. They then become asteroids. Sometimes, they break up violently and crash into a planet or into the Sun.

Some comets, known as short-period comets, make elongated orbits that regularly bring them near the Sun. One of the most famous is Halley's comet, which returns about every 76 years and was studied by space probes on its last appearance in 1986. Astronomers think that in a zone very distant from the Sun and therefore very cold, there are billions of comets. According to this theory, the comets we see come from this zone. Preserved intact, as if in a refrigerator, they help astronomers to understand how the solar system was formed.

Meteors and meteorites

Every day, the Earth passes through a multitude of space debris attracted by its gravitational pull. The smallest pieces burn up in the **atmosphere** and fall as fine dust. As they burn up, these pieces of matter create beautiful luminous trails in the sky. These are **meteors**, also called **shooting stars**.

The heaviest pieces of debris sometimes explode in the atmosphere but do not burn up completely. Pieces fall to the ground to be found as **meteorites**. Some scientists believe that the impact of an enormous meteorite 65 million years ago caused the disappearance of the dinosaurs. At certain times of the year, for example, around 12 August or 21 October, the Earth moves across the orbits of comets along which swarms of debris have accumulated. When this debris hits the Earth's atmosphere it turns into a "shower" of shooting stars. The Earth gets bigger by about 10,000 tons a year because of matter that it "sweeps up" in space. ☐

Halley's comet seen from the Earth

The planet Jupiter struck by a comet

In July 1994, astronomers directly monitored the fall onto Jupiter of fragments of a comet named Shoemaker-Levy 9. They recorded 21 separate fragments, forming a string more than 1 million kilometers in length, colliding with Jupiter at more than 200,000 km/h (124,000 mph). The hardest impact produced a dark spot larger than the Earth.

Meteor Crater

The greatest meteorite impact known on Earth is marked by Meteor Crater in Arizona. The crater has a diameter of 1,200 m (3,937 ft) and a depth of 180 m (590 ft). The meteorite that hollowed out this crater probably fell to Earth around 50,000 years ago.

Stars

and galaxies

The Sun

The Sun is the closest star to the Earth, so astronomers can observe it more easily than any other. They can discover what it is made of and how it affects our planet.

❍ **aurora:** luminous displays in the sky above the Earth's polar regions.

❍ **chromosphere:** layer of the Sun's atmosphere above the photosphere.

❍ **corona:** outer layer of the Sun's atmosphere, extending beyond the chromosphere.

❍ **photosphere:** luminous surface layer of the Sun.

❍ **prominence:** gas shot out from the chromosphere into the corona.

❍ **solar activity:** all the phenomena observed on the Sun, such as sunspots.

❍ **solar flare:** sudden discharge of energy in the chromo-sphere and the corona above an area of sunspots.

❍ **solar wind:** constant flow of atomic particles streaming out from the Sun.

❍ **spicule:** thin, spiky geyser of gas. Spicules make up the Sun's chromosphere.

❍ **star:** a very hot gaseous body in space that produces and gives off light.

❍ **Sun:** the star around which the Earth and the other planets of the solar system revolve.

The **Sun** is the star we know best because it is close to us, in space terms. Astronomers can distinguish fine details on its surface, as small as 150 km (93 mi) across. Compared to the Earth, the Sun is gigantic: 1,300,000 planets like ours could be contained within its volume, and 109 Earths could be lined up along its diameter. The Sun is an enormous sphere of hot gases, with a mass 300,000 times greater than that of the Earth. The gravity on its surface is about 28 times stronger than on Earth.

Nevertheless, the Sun is a very ordinary star. There is nothing exceptional about its size and mass. Studying such a commonplace star helps astronomers to understand other stars.

The photosphere

The Sun's blinding light comes from a layer less than 300 km (186 mi) deep, the **photosphere**. The photosphere gives the impression that the Sun has a clearly defined edge. Its temperature is around 6,000°C (over 10,000°F). Viewed through a telescope, the Sun looks like a honeycomb of small brilliant cells, or granules, in continual movement. Each granule is a bubble of gas the size of France. They rise up, transform and disappear within ten minutes.

In some places on the surface of the Sun, dark spots can be seen. These are known as sunspots. Asian observers noticed their

An ultraviolet image of the Sun, showing an immense prominence (left)

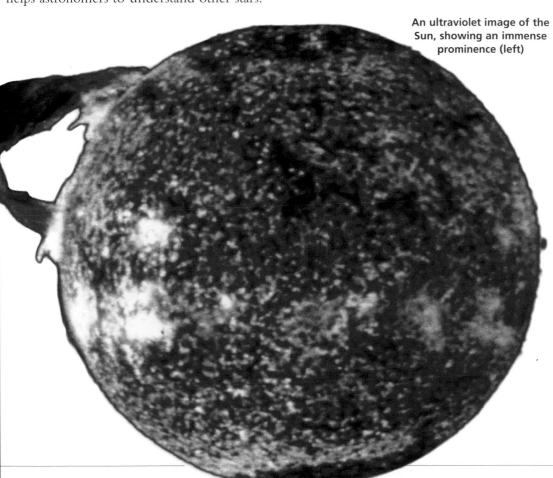

existence over 2,000 years ago. Following the invention of telescopes, sunspots were studied in detail. Observing them day after day has shown that sunspots are not always in the same place. Their movement proves that the Sun rotates on its axis, taking about a month.

The chromosphere and the corona

During a total eclipse of the Sun, when the Sun's blinding disk disappears behind the Moon, a thin bright pink layer becomes visible around the Sun. This is the **chromosphere**, and above it an irregular silvery halo, the **corona**, can be seen. The chromosphere and the corona are the outer layers of the Sun. They form the solar atmosphere. Normally, they cannot be seen because they are a lot less bright than the photosphere. The chromosphere extends about 5,000 km (3,100 mi) above the Sun's surface and teems with geysers of very hot gases, called **spicules**. The temperature of a spicule increases with altitude, reaching 20,000°C (36,000°F). The corona surrounds the chromosphere. It gets thinner as it extends into space and has no clear outer limit. The corona is also extremely hot—over 1 million degrees C (1,800,000°F). With special instruments, some areas of the chromosphere can be seen from time to time to become suddenly intensely bright. These are **solar flares**. Immense projections of gas, known as **prominences**, rise through the chromosphere and the corona. When seen shooting from the Sun, prominences look like dark threads. Through the corona, a flow of very rapid particles escapes from the Sun all the time. This is the **solar wind**.

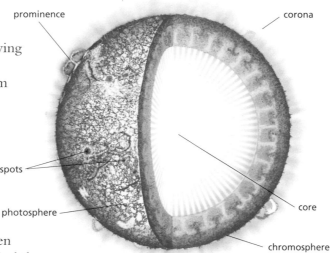

A cutaway diagram of the Sun

Inside the Sun

The Sun's interior cannot be seen, but the study of the Sun's surface and outer layers gives astronomers information about its internal structure. Although it contains all the simple elements identified on Earth, 98 percent of its mass is made up of the gases hydrogen and helium: 73 percent hydrogen and 25 percent helium. Toward its center, or core, the Sun becomes hotter and hotter, and matter more compressed. At the very center the temperature is around 15 million degrees C (59 million degrees F), and the pressure is 100 million times that on Earth. In this furnace, hydrogen atoms combine in groups of four to form helium atoms. This reaction releases heat and light, and causes the Sun to shine. Every second in the heart of the Sun, 400 million tons of hydrogen are transformed into helium. It takes the light energy from the center of the Sun 2 million years to reach the surface! ☐

A sunspot

Sunspots appear dark because they are about 1,500° to 2,000°C (2,700° to 3,600°F) cooler than surrounding areas. They are often seen in pairs, which behave like the two poles of an enormous magnet. They can remain visible for several weeks. The number of sunspots observed varies over a cycle of about 11 years.

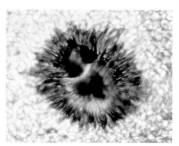

The solar corona

This immense gaseous envelope extends several million kilometers from the edge of the Sun. Its appearance varies with the cycles of solar activity. Round and regular when the Sun is very active, it bristles with jets of gaseous matter during periods of solar "calm."

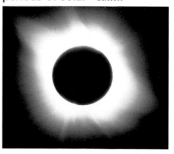

Typical solar prominences

Observing solar activity and the Sun

A solar flare

When a solar flare occurs, an enormous amount of energy stored in the Sun's chromosphere and corona is suddenly released. Matter is expelled from the corona, and atomic particles are accelerated at high speeds into interplanetary space. X rays and radio waves are emitted at the same time and,

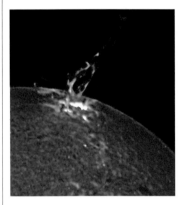

in the case of the most intense flares, visible light. When these particles come near Earth and fall into the atmosphere, mainly above the poles, they trigger auroras. They also disturb the transmission of radio waves around the world. Sometimes they even damage electricity networks. In New York, in May 1969 and April 1972, they caused spectacular power failures.

New astronomical telescopes have made it easier for us to observe the disturbances of the Sun: the sunspots within the photosphere, the flares, **prominences** and threads in the **chromosphere**, and the jets of gas in the **corona**. We know now that these phenomena are linked parts of **solar activity**. Their frequency and intensity vary over a period of around 11 years, during which the number of sunspots passes through a minimum and a maximum. The next maximum is expected around the year 2011. Solar activity is still something of a mystery, though we know it is associated with the magnetism and rotation of the Sun.

The Sun and the Earth

When the Sun becomes more active, its surface is covered with sunspots and there are more **solar flares**. The flares release into space enormous blasts of invisible radiation, such as x rays, ultraviolet rays and radio waves. At the same time, there is an intense outward flow of electrically charged particles. This is known as the **solar wind**. The particles with the highest levels of energy reach the Earth in a few hours and collect around the planet, forming belts of radiation. Other particles take from one to two days to reach us. They are deflected by the Earth's magnetic shield, the magnetosphere, and then attracted by its magnetic poles. When these particles fall into the atmosphere they produce the colored polar lights known in the northern hemisphere as the aurora borealis and in the southern hemisphere as the aurora australis. These lights are like immense veils, reddish or greenish in color, swaying in the sky.

Influence on climate

Variations in solar activity seem to affect the Earth's climate. For example, between 1645

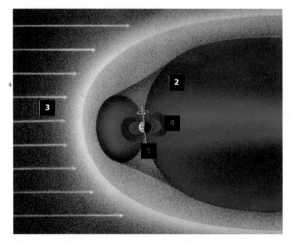

The Earth's magnetosphere. It forms around the Earth (1) a kind of magnetic shield (2) that diverts the solar wind (3), a flow of particles emitted by the Sun. The most highly charged particles collect around the Earth in radiation belts (4).

and 1715, no sunspots were observed, and this period coincided with the coldest years of a "little ice age" when temperatures in Europe were abnormally low. By contrast, since 1900, the Sun has been very active and the temperature on Earth has increased slightly. Many links between solar activity and periods of cold or heat waves on the Earth have been discovered. However, the exact way in which changes in solar activity influence the climate is unknown.

A polar aurora

Solar observatories

Observatories for the study of the Sun have been set up around the world, for example, in the United States (Kitt Peak, Sacramento Peak, Big Bear), in Spain (Canary Islands), in France (Meudon), in Russia (Crimea), in Japan (Mitaka, Norikura, Toyokowa), and in Australia (Culgoora). Such observatories have instruments designed to observe and analyze sunlight.

Telescopes used to study the Sun have very large focal lengths, up to 100 m (330 ft), making it possible to achieve large images of the Sun (tens of centimeters, or a foot or more in diameter). These telescopes are installed in towers so that the sunlight is collected high above the ground. This is necessary to obtain clear images, because near the ground, heat causes air turbulence that blurs images. Using a system of mirrors, the Sun is tracked across the sky, and its light is constantly projected onto the telescope.

The spectroheliograph and coronograph

The spectroheliograph provides images of the Sun in a single color. Often, the light chosen is that of a red-band radiation of hydrogen. The coronograph is a special telescope that makes it possible to mask the blinding disk of the Sun, so that the corona can be observed at times other than those of total solar eclipses. To gain the best performance from this instrument, it must be set up at high altitude, where the atmosphere is very clear. Special radio telescopes are used to record the radio waves emitted by the Sun. The other invisible radiation from the Sun (such as ultraviolet rays and x rays) is studied using instruments installed on satellites and spacecraft.

Arched solar prominences

Observing sunspots

A simple method for observing sunspots has been used since the invention of the refracting telescope. The Sun's image is projected onto a white screen placed at the focus of either a refracting or reflecting telescope. Sunspots appear as small dark spots on the screen.

An underground laboratory

In the Gran Sasso laboratory in northern Italy, there is an enormous underground detector. Deep under a mountain, it collects neutrinos, tiny atomic particles. From these particles, astronomers learn more about the interior of the Sun.

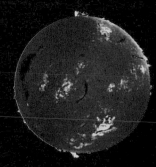

Auroras

The northern lights are familiar to people living close to or within the Arctic Circle. Polar auroras are among the most beautiful sights in the sky. Their appearance often resembles luminous reddish or greenish curtains, stretching and fluttering over vast distances. The aurora borealis, or northern lights, can be seen in the northern hemisphere, and it is the aurora australis that can be seen in the southern hemisphere. Polar auroras can sometimes be seen farther away from the poles, in temperate regions. The first scientific description of the aurora borealis was given in 1621, by a French astronomer named Pierre Gassendi.

The stars

○ **black dwarf:** a white dwarf star that at the end of its life, no longer gives off light.

○ **black hole:** an area of space where the gravitational force is so great that nothing can break free from it, not even light; possibly a collapsing star.

○ **globule:** a dark, nearly spherical cloud of matter between stars, one of the first stages in the formation of a new star.

○ **neutron star:** a very small star. Its matter is so compressed that it is reduced to a "pulp" of atomic particles called neutrons.

○ **protostar:** first noticeable stage in the development of a star.

○ **red giant:** an old star. All the hydrogen in its center has become helium, and the star swells as it cools.

○ **supergiant:** a very big bright star.

○ **supernova:** a massive star that explodes; also the explosion itself.

○ **white dwarf:** a small star, very dense and faint, at the last stage in its evolution.

Like living things, stars are born, grow, change, and finally die. This process unfolds over a very long time: millions or even billions of years.

At first glance, all stars seem identical. In fact, they are often very different. To put together each star's "profile," astronomers study starlight, which is the clue to the star's nature.

The brightness of stars

In the night sky, some stars appear brighter than others. A star's brightness depends not only on the quantity of light that it emits, but also on its distance. Brightness is expressed by a number, the star's magnitude. The brighter a star is, the smaller the magnitude number. A star that is one magnitude less than another is two-and-a-half times brighter. One that is five magnitudes less is one hundred times brighter. The faintest stars to be seen with the unaided eye are magnitude 6.

With binoculars, it is possible to see a star of magnitude 9. With the most powerful modern telescopes, stars of magnitude 26 can be detected: this is 100 million times less bright than the faintest star visible to the unaided eye. To compare the luminosity of stars (the quantity of light they send out into space) astronomers have defined an absolute magnitude, independent of distance.

Color and temperature

When you look carefully at the stars, you notice that they are not all the same color. Among the brightest, Sirius is white, Vega is bluish, Aldebaran and Antares reddish. This is due to greater or lesser degrees of heat of their surfaces. When a bar of iron is heated, it changes color as its temperature increases. At first reddish, it will turn orange, then yellow and finally white. Likewise, the color of a star tells us about its surface temperature. A white star is hotter than a red star but cooler than a blue star. The hottest stars are blue: their surface temperatures at times exceeds 30,000°C (54,000°F). Besides indicating temperature, starlight tells us about the star's chemical composition and its movement. Everything we know about the stars we have learned from their light. The information is contained in each star's spectrum, obtained by splitting its light into different colors.

Stars are very far away

If you observe a star that is fairly close to the Earth, at intervals of six months, you will find

SURFACE TEMPERATURE (in °C)

| | 20,000 | 10,000 | 7,5 |

10,000

blue supergiants

10,000

100

1

LUMINOSITY IN RELATION TO THE SUN

white dwarves

0.01

0.0001

Stars and nebulas in the Milky Way

that it appears in a new position in the night sky. Using the diameter of the Earth's orbit (which is 300 million km or 186 million mi), it is possible to work out the angle by which the star seems to be displaced. Divide this angle by two, and the star's distance can be found. This method can be used only for a few thousand "close" stars.

For the rest, the angles to be measured are too small, and their distance from us has to be calculated using other methods. Even the closest stars are so far away that kilometers or miles become meaningless. A much bigger unit, the light-year, is used instead. This is the distance that light travels in a vacuum in one year. Light travels at roughly 300,000 km a second (186,000 mi/s). In one year, it travels almost 10 trillion km (6.2 trillion mi). The closest star is 4 light-years away. Named Proxima (Latin for "closest") Centauri, it is in the constellation Centaurus, which can be seen only from the southern hemisphere. Light reaching us from distant stars left them hundreds or even thousands of years ago. ☐

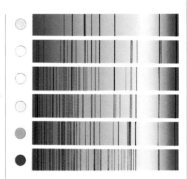

The six main types of star spectra

The spectra (plural of spectrum) of stars vary with their color. Each bright or dark line in the spectrum signifies the presence of a chemical element in or around the star. This is the star's "identity card."

The constellation Orion

Orion is one of the most beautiful constellations in the night sky. In this picture, the different colors of its stars can be seen: Betelgeuse (top left) is red, Rigel (bottom right) is blue.

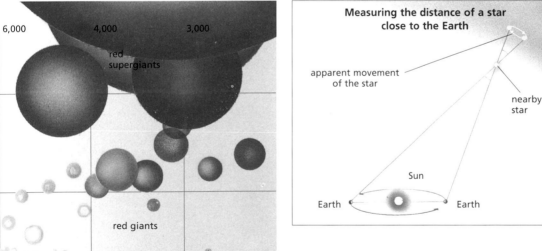

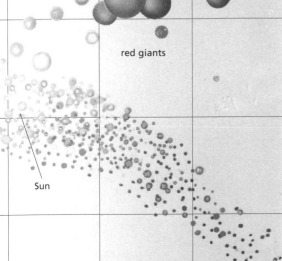

6,000   4,000   3,000

red supergiants

red giants

Sun

Measuring the distance of a star close to the Earth

apparent movement of the star

nearby star

Sun

Earth   Earth

The Hertzsprung-Russell diagram

Two astronomers, Ejnar Hertzsprung of Denmark and H. N. Russell of the United States, classified the stars by spectra and luminosity. The most numerous stars are those like our Sun, and in the diagram such stars lie along a diagonal, the main sequence or series. There are also giants and supergiants, which are much brighter, and white dwarfs, which are much fainter. ■

A partial view of the molecular cloud Rho Ophiuchi

From birth to maturity

A star nursery

The Rosette nebula (shown below is its central area) lies in the constellation Monoceros and is an immense star nursery. It contains a huge number of dark globules, stars in their formative stages that do not yet shine. The nebula includes a cluster of three very hot young stars (less than a million years old). The radiation from these stars has swept the gas and dust from the center of the nebula and scattered it through space at tremendous speeds. The light from this vast cloud of interstellar material began its journey to us about 1500 BC.

The birth of a star takes place over millions of years, in stages. Within a cloud of molecule, **globules** of matter form that become **protostars**, and then stars.

Molecular clouds

In space, there are immense clouds of gas and dust known as **nebulas**. In some of these clouds, matter becomes dense and concentrated, forming molecular clouds. These clouds are so big that light takes dozens of years to cross them, and their mass may be several hundred thousand times that of the Sun.

Cloud matter is very cold, at temperatures around –250°C (–418°F). They are called molecular clouds because the gas they contain is in the form of molecules, a combination of atoms. Each cloud is in delicate equilibrium. An external disturbance, such as the shock wave from an exploding nearby star, can break this equilibrium. Part of the cloud then collapses under its own weight. Its matter begins to contract. The cloud breaks up into small clusters of material.

Globules

The debris from the breakup of the molecular cloud contracts and slowly changes into huge, dark spheres or **globules**. A typical globule is as big as the solar system, with a mass ranging from 1 to 200 times that of the Sun. It is still a very cold and dark body. Gradually, as it shrinks, it becomes denser and hotter. It changes into a **protostar**, and begins to shine.

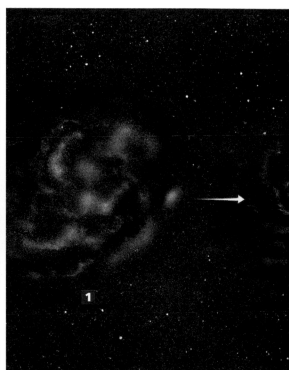

The Pleiades, a cluster of young stars

Protostars

The matter in the protostar continues to contract. Protostars appear to be enveloped in a cocoon of gas. They shine, but only irregularly. Jets of gas shoot out at enormous speed from their poles. When the center temperature reaches 10 million degrees C, nuclear reactions begin. A star is born. The time needed for a protostar to become a star depends on its mass. It takes 30 million years for a protostar to become a star as big as our Sun, but less than 300,000 years for a star 10 times more massive.

Young stars

Once they begin to shine, stars get their energy from the fusion of hydrogen into helium in their centers. The length of this process varies according to the star's mass. For a star like the Sun, the process lasts for 10 billion years. For a star 3 times more massive, it is complete in 500 million years, and for a star 30 times more massive, it takes only 6 million years.

Stages in the formation of a star

Part of a molecular cloud in which matter is more concentrated begins to collapse under its own weight (1). It forms a spinning disk that is hotter and more dense in the center (2). Here a protostar ignites and releases jets of matter (3). The protostar becomes hotter and brighter (4), then nuclear reactions are set off and the star is born (5).

Double stars

Often where we see one star there are in fact two stars very close to each other. Gravitational force keeps them from pulling apart, and they orbit around each other, as a double star or binary. Algol (ß Perseus) is an eclipsing binary. It is formed by a very bright blue star and a larger yellow star that is less bright. Its brightness diminishes sharply when the yellow star moves in

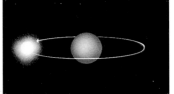

front of the blue star and less notably when the blue star passes in front of the yellow. These variations in luminosity follow a 2,867-day cycle. Besides binaries, triple stars, quadruples, and larger groups exist.

3　　　　4　　　　5

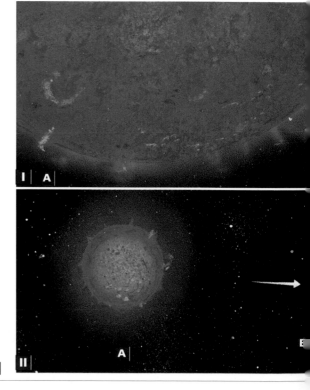

The planetary nebula Helix

Old age and death

The supernova SN 1987A

The star Sk 69202, a supergiant between 15 and 20 times more massive than the Sun, was located in the Great Magellanic Cloud. This is a small galaxy close to ours, visible from the southern

hemisphere. Astronomers paid little attention to this star until it exploded on 24 January 1987. Its brightness increased abruptly and it became the most brilliant supernova seen for 400 years. The explosion actually took place around 170,000 years ago!

When there is no longer enough hydrogen in the center of a star, its core contracts and it becomes hotter. There is still plenty of hydrogen in the star's outer layers, and this goes on changing into helium. The star swells and turns red. It becomes a **red giant**, from 10 to 100 times bigger than the Sun. In the center further nuclear reactions are set off, and the helium in the star's core is converted into carbon. From this point, the length of the star's final stage depends on its mass.

White dwarfs

The lightest stars, with a mass less than 1.4 times greater than the Sun's, at first become unstable. They shine erratically, and their outer layers are ejected into space. These layers form a bubble of expanding gas, called a planetary **nebula**, around the star. When all the helium in the star's core has turned into carbon, the star again contracts. But it is not now hot enough to unleash further nuclear reactions. It becomes a **white dwarf**, a small star no bigger than the Earth but so dense that a teaspoonful of its matter weighs a ton. The star gradually cools, losing its brightness, until only a **black dwarf**, too cold to shine, is left.

The final stages in the life of a star

A massive star becomes a red supergiant (A), which explodes into a supernova (B). Its core then transforms into either a neutron star (C1) or a black hole (C2).
A less massive star, like our Sun, changes into a red giant (A). It expels its outer layers, which form a planetary nebula (B). Then the star becomes a white dwarf (C), which fades away, leaving a black dwarf (D).

Supernovae

The most massive stars produce heavy chemical elements, including iron. They expand and become **supergiants**, as much as 1,000 times bigger than the Sun. Inside these giant stars are layers of different gases, which become cooler and less dense toward the outer edge. Suddenly, an explosion scatters the star's material into space, in a display like cosmic fireworks. The star flares with the brilliance of 10 billion Suns. This is called a **supernova**, because from the Earth, it looks as if a very bright new star has appeared in the sky. After the explosion, only the core of the star remains. Depending on its mass, this becomes either a **neutron star** or a **black hole**.

Neutron stars

The explosion of a supergiant does not destroy it completely but lays bare its iron heart. This

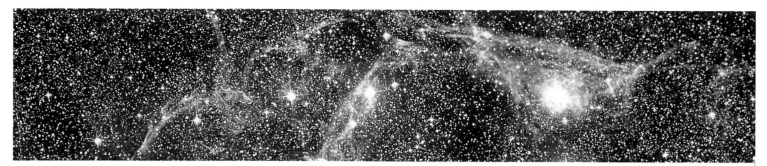

The remains of a supernova, the Veil nebula

is compressed fantastically, to a small ball about 20 km (12 mi) across but immensely massive (up to 500 million tons per cubic centimeter). To transform the Earth into a body as dense, it would be necessary, without changing its mass, to squash the planet into a ball 30 m (less than 100 ft) in diameter. In what remains of the star, matter is so compressed that all the atoms are crushed. The star becomes a "soup" of atomic particles called neutrons. It has become a neutron star, so small and faint that it can easily remain unnoticed. However, astronomers can identify one type of neutron star, known as a pulsar, from the pulsating radio waves and other radiation it gives out.

Black holes

If the core of an exploding star is heavy enough, it changes finally into something even stranger than a neutron star—a black hole, only a few kilometers across but of an unimaginable density. A black hole has such a huge gravitational pull that it swallows up anything that passes too close forever. Nothing, neither matter nor radiation, can escape from it. A black hole even retains its own light, hence its name. Although it is invisible, astronomers can detect a black hole because of the disturbances it causes all around it.

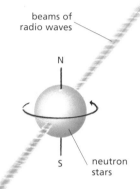

beams of radio waves

N

S

neutron stars

Pulsars

Pulsars are neutron stars that rotate very rapidly on their axes and give off a beam of radio waves or other forms of radiation in one direction. This beam sweeps through space like the flashing light of a police car. If the Earth crosses the beam's path, the pulsar can be detected. The beam disappears momentarily and is picked up again when the star has made a complete rotation, a few seconds or a fraction of a second later. Several hundred neutron stars have been found in this way. They are called pulsars ("pulsing stars") because rays from them reach us at very regular intervals, as if the star is pulsating regularly. The first pulsars were discovered in 1967 at the radio observatory in Cambridge, England.

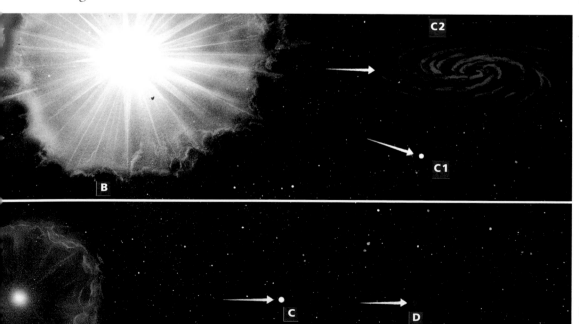

The Horsehead Nebula

When the night sky is observed through a reflecting telescope or a refracting telescope, wonders hidden from the unaided eye are revealed. Among such wonders are nebulas, immense clouds of gas and dust dispersed between the stars. One of the most famous is the Horsehead Nebula, so called because of its shape. It is a cloud of interstellar dust, outlined against another, brighter, nebula. Visible in the direction of the constellation Orion, and 1,100 light-years away from us, it stretches over an expanse of space some 3 light-years wide.

The galaxies

Across the universe are strewn billions of stars and nebulas of gas and dust, grouped together in immense islands of matter: the galaxies. Our galaxy, containing the solar system, traces the Milky Way across the sky.

◐ **active galaxy:** special galaxy with a nucleus that gives off an exceptional amount of energy.

◐ **cluster (of galaxies):** group of

from a few dozen to a few thousand galaxies.

◐ **galaxy:** vast mass of stars and interstellar matter (gas and dust), held together through mutual attraction: each is an island of matter in the universe.

◐ **halo:** spherical region around the disk of a spiral galaxy, in which old stars are massed in globular clusters.

◐ **nebula:** cloud of gas and dust in space, extending between the stars of a galaxy.

◐ **nucleus (of a galaxy):** central area of a galaxy, where the matter is most concentrated and which gives off the most light.

◐ **quasar:** very luminous star, smaller than a galaxy, located beyond our galaxy.

◐ **radio galaxy:** a galaxy that is a very powerful source of radio waves.

◐ **supercluster:** cluster of clusters of galaxies.

In the second half of the 18th century, William Herschel, an astronomer born in Germany but living in England, began to construct large telescopes. Using these instruments, he made many observations of the night sky and counted the stars he saw spread in different directions. He discovered that the Sun is part of a vast star group, flattened in shape, for which he suggested the name, the **galaxy**. The Milky Way is its visible trail in the sky. Since the beginning of the 20th century, more powerful telescopes have shown us that the universe is studded with millions of galaxies, all more or less like our own.

Our galaxy

After many observations, astronomers have pieced together the structure, shape and size of our galaxy. Its main part (including two-thirds of its total mass) is an immense disk about 100,000 light-years in diameter, although only 1,000 to 2,000 light-years in average depth. In this disk, matter is concentrated along three or four spiraling arms. This is why our galaxy is described as a spiral galaxy. The arms are the areas where new stars are formed. The Sun is located on the edge of one arm, roughly 30,000 light-years from the center of the galaxy. In the center of the disk is the bulging **nucleus**, about 15,000 light-years long and 5,000 light-years thick. This is the densest area of the galaxy. The bulge is made up of old stars. The central nucleus is hidden behind nebulas of gas and dust and can be studied only though the invisible radiation that it emits, including infrared and radio waves. The nucleus conceals a vast concentration of matter. This may be a huge cluster of stars, or even an enormous black hole.

Star clusters

Groups of stars formed at the same time make up **clusters**. Study of our galaxy has revealed two types of star clusters. Within the disk there are groups of hundreds of separate young stars: these are open, or galactic, clusters. Around the disk, spread in an immense spherical **halo**, are enormous "clumps" of very old stars: these are globular clusters. Each cluster may contain several hundred stars. In the central area of globular clusters, the stars are so tightly packed together that they cannot be individually distinguished.

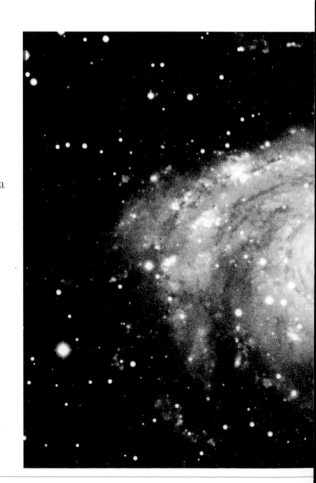

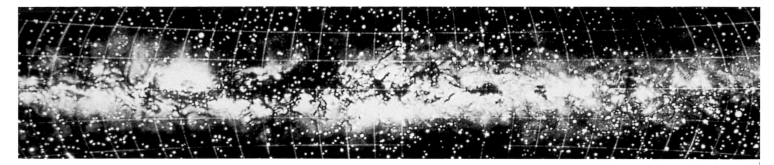

The nebulas

Matter spread among the stars forms **nebulas**. These are basically made up of hydrogen—the most common element in the universe—but also contain vast quantities of dust. Many different kinds of nebulas exist. Diffuse nebulas give out light when they are located near hot stars, like the Orion Nebula. Other nebulas can be detected only from the radio waves given out by their hydrogen atoms. Dark nebulas do not give out light but absorb it from the star located behind them. They stand out as elaborate shadows against the starlit sky. The Horsehead Nebula, in the constellation Orion, is a fine example. In some nebulas, stars are being born. When the matter in a nebula is concentrated enough, the atoms join to form molecules. The nebula becomes a molecular cloud from which stars develop. This is happening in the nebula Rho Ophiuchi. Other nebulas are the remains of old stars. These are planetary nebulas and the remains of supernovae. Planetary nebulas are bubbles of gas expelled by small-mass stars that have become unstable toward the end of their life. They break up in space over tens of thousands of years. The remains of supernovae are the debris left by the explosion of massive stars. Their material is scattered at great speed, following a shock wave that compresses and heats interstellar space. The most famous supernova is the Crab Nebula, in the constellation Taurus, the result of an exploding star observed in 1054 by the Chinese. The star flared so brightly that it could be seen in daylight for three weeks. □

The spiral galaxy NGC 2997: it is the same shape as our galaxy.

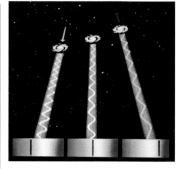

The Doppler effect

The radiation spectrum of a light source in space can be used to find out whether the source is approaching or moving away, and to measure its distance. If the source is approaching us, the lines of the spectrum are shifted toward the blue band. If it is moving away, the lines of the spectrum are shifted toward the red band.

Edwin Hubble (1889–1953)

Hubble's observations changed our view of the universe. He discovered the galaxies and, by studying their spectra, concluded that the universe is expanding.

61

M104, the Sombrero Galaxy

The other galaxies

The shape of galaxies

In 1926, Hubble suggested classifying galaxies by their shape: spiral (1), elliptical (2) and irregular (3). About 80 percent of galaxies are spiral,

1

2

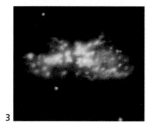

3

15 percent are elliptical and 3 percent irregular. About 2 percent of galaxies are peculiar and do not fit into any of these major groups. Spiral galaxies are called "normal" when their arms branch out directly from a central nucleus and "barred" when the arms branch out from the ends of a bar-shaped nucleus. Our galaxy is a normal spiral galaxy.

The astronomer William Herschel (1738–1822) and other scientists and philosophers of his time, such as Thomas Wright (1711–1786) and Emmanuel Kant (1724-1804), believed that our galaxy is not unique and that the universe is filled with similar systems. The work of Edwin Hubble (1889-1953) finally gave proof of other galaxies.

Discovery of the galaxies

In 1924, using the great telescope of the Mount Wilson observatory in California, Edwin Hubble pinpointed individual stars in what was then called the great Andromeda "nebula." What most astronomers had thought to be just a vast cloud of gas was thus revealed to be a gigantic group of stars and interstellar material—a **galaxy**. A great number of other galaxies were then identified. Now, tens of million are known. Galaxies close to one another are mutually attracted by a force strong enough to deform them. There are even galaxies linked by bridges of matter.

Above: the barred spiral galaxy, NGC 1365 ▲   Below

Active galaxies

Certain galaxies (fewer than 5 percent) are "active" or "active nucleus" galaxies. The **nucleus** of such galaxies emits a thousand times more energy than those of ordinary galaxies, and is an intense source of x rays, ultraviolet rays and gamma rays. The effects of these rays make surrounding matter intensely hot and disturbed by violent movements. Radio waves and a concentrated beam of very fast electrons are sent out. Some **active galaxies** are known as **radio galaxies**, because most of their emissions are radio waves. Each radio galaxy gives off around 1 billion times more radiation in the form of radio waves than an ordinary galaxy.

M31 (NGC 224), the great spiral galaxy in Andromeda

e elliptical galaxy NGC 5128 (radio galaxy Centaurus A) ▼

Quasars

Since 1963, astronomers have been identifying objects that appear to be very bright nuclei of distant active galaxies. Since they resemble stars, and since the first to be discovered emitted large amounts of radio waves, they were called **quasars**, from the expression *quasi stellar radio source*.

Why do quasars emit so much energy? Astronomers now think that a quasar harbors in its center a gigantic **black hole**, of a mass some 100 million times that of the Sun. Before being engulfed by this black hole, the gas surrounding it swirls and becomes very hot. The gas then emits the very intense radiation that makes the unbelievable energy released by quasars. Astronomers consider quasars to be the most distant objects in space yet found. The lines of their spectrum are very markedly shifted toward red, which suggests that they are located at an extreme distance. From their apparent brightness, they must be 100 to 1,000 times more luminous than the galaxies, yet they are 100 times smaller.

Their suspected remoteness make quasars a source of information on the distant past of the universe. Light from them has traveled for billions of years in space before reaching us. From it, we see what the universe was like billions of years ago. □

Quasar 3C273

Quasar 3C273 is one of the closest to us, at two billion light-years away. It was the first quasar to be measured successfully by studying its spectrum. This photograph, taken by the Hubble Space Telescope, shows the quasar with a jet of swiftly moving material emerging from its nucleus.

Colliding galaxies

These are two interacting galaxies. Two strands of matter branch out from them, like the antennae of an insect. Each strand extends over 100,000 light-years. These galaxies are located 48 million light-years away.

The Large Magellanic Cloud

Clusters and superclusters

The dark matter mystery

Research suggests that there is a large corona of dark matter beyond the disk of our galaxy. Studies of the movement of galaxies in clusters have led astronomers to conclude that

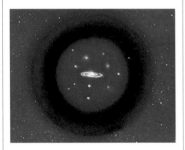

there is ten times more dark matter than luminous matter in the universe. This invisible matter could be formed, for example, by stars that are burned out or too small to ignite, by great clouds of very cold gas, or even by atomic particles. Astronomers are trying to prove the existence of this dark matter, to discover if it is indeed an important part of the universe.

It is rare for galaxies to be alone in space. Usually they form into groups, known as **clusters** and **superclusters**. To understand the structure of the universe it is important to study the distribution of clusters over very great distances in space.

Clusters of galaxies

Most galaxies belong to groups of one to several dozen galaxies or to clusters that may include several thousand galaxies. The force with which the galaxies of a group or cluster attract each other is enough to stop them from breaking away. Our galaxy belongs to the Local Group, a small cluster with some 30 members. This cluster also contains Andromeda's M31 galaxy, which was the first to be identified after our own, and the only one visible to the unaided eye from the northern hemisphere. M31 is a spiral galaxy like the Milky Way and is located 2.4 million light-years away.

Superclusters

Several tens of thousands of galaxy clusters have been identified. They are often grouped in immense clusters of clusters, or superclusters, extending across 100 million light-years or more. The Local Group and all the nearby galaxies are included in the Local Supercluster, which stretches about 50 million light-years away.

The most spectacular concentration of galaxies seen in the northern hemisphere of the sky was detected in 1989. It is called the "Great Wall," and it is a chain of clusters and superclusters creating a formidable barrier of galaxies 500 million light-years long, 200 million light-years wide, and 15 million light-years deep. Recent research suggests that our galaxy is in the grip of an enormous concentration of matter pulling it and disturbing its movement. This Great Attractor apparently extends over about 250 million light-years in the direction of the

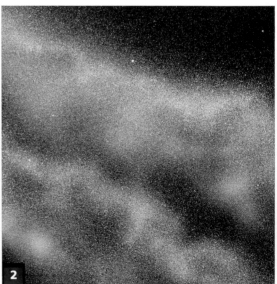

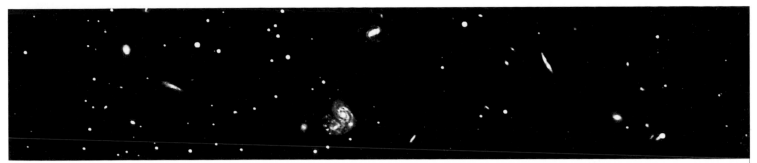

The cluster of galaxies in the constellation Hercules

On this map of a section of the sky, each bright point represents a galaxy. Some zones are empty and others are densely packed.

The structure of the universe

Some regions of space are practically empty of galaxies. The first of these great voids was detected in 1981, in the direction of the constellation Boötes, and is 300 million light-years across. Perhaps groups of galaxies (clusters and superclusters) are arranged on the walls of gigantic cells, with their interiors empty of galaxies. The structure of the universe would then be like that of a sponge, or a mass of soap bubbles. ☐

Local Group and Local Supercluster

With its near neighbors, our galaxy forms the Local Group of galaxies. This cluster is 7 million light-years long and has a mass estimated at 650 billion times that of the Sun. Of special interest in the group are two small irregular galaxies that are satellites of our own, the Large Magellanic Cloud and the Small Magellanic Cloud, as well as the famous M31 galaxy in Andromeda. The Local Group is itself part of an even more enormous flattened gathering of galaxies, some 100 million light-years long, known as the Local Supercluster. Our galaxy is on the edge of this system, some 50 million light-years from the center.

constellations Hydra and Centaurus (visible in the southern hemisphere). It seems to have a phenomenal mass, equal to 30 trillion times that of our galaxy. Its center would be 150 million light-years away.

The solar system in the universe

The Earth and the other planets of the solar system revolve around a star, the Sun (1). The Sun is one of 100 billion stars in our galaxy (2, 3). Our galaxy forms with about 30 of its neighbors a small galaxy cluster, the Local Group (4). The Local Group is part of a vast concentration of galaxies, the Local Supercluster (5). ■

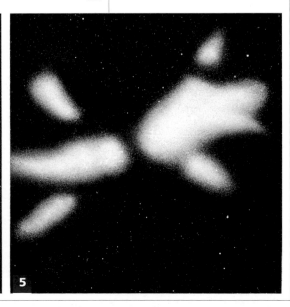

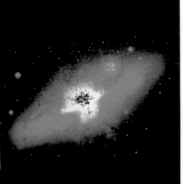

From

Many scientists believe that everything began some 15 billion years ago. The universe was then incredibly hot and dense, and contained only energy. Suddenly, there was a cataclysmic explosion: the Big Bang.

the Big Bang to

The Big Bang shook this hot, dense furnace and began its expansion. Ever since, the universe has been expanding and cooling. A few minutes after the Big Bang, the main constituents of the matter in the universe were formed: hydrogen and helium. Light did not begin to be generated for another 400,000 years.

From particles of galaxies

The primitive universe was a hot "soup" of **particles** moving in all directions at speeds near the speed of light. As it cooled, some particles disappeared and others replaced them. In less than 15 minutes, **nuclear fusion** led to the formation of light **atomic nuclei**, such as those of hydrogen and helium. These first eventful minutes were followed by a long settled period, during which the first atoms formed. While it continued to swell and cool, the universe remained for a long time in darkness. Not until 300,000 to 400,000 years later, when the temperature dropped below 3,000°C (5,400°F), was light freely produced. Several hundred million years passed before the first **galaxies** were formed, from small "lumps" in the gaseous matter. Exactly how they formed is still a mystery. Astronomers have developed the **Big Bang** theory from studying the light emitted from galaxies. Except for light coming from the

nearest galaxies, all light from galaxies is reddened when it reaches us. The lines of its spectra are systematically shifted from their normal positions toward the red band. The more marked this redshift, the more distant the galaxy. A simple conclusion from this is that all galaxies are moving away from one another because the entire universe is expanding. The Big Bang theory suggests that an initial explosion caused this **expansion**.

The Big Bang theory has its opponents, however. Some astronomers reject the idea that the universe began in this way. Even so, it remains the simplest theory and the one that best fits with scientific observation.

Radiation clues

In 1965, two American radio astronomers, Arno Penzias and Robert Wilson, accidentally detected a strange radio wave emission from space. They later demonstrated that this radiation came from all directions and not from any one star or star group. The Big Bang theory could explain this discovery. The mysterious radiation is a leftover from the universe's original heat. It matches the radiation emitted by the universe 300,000 to 400,000 years after the Big

Big Bang

FORMATION
OF PARTICLES

FORMATION
OF ATOMIC NUCLEI

FORMATION
OF ATOMS

0.000001 second

100 seconds

300,000 yea

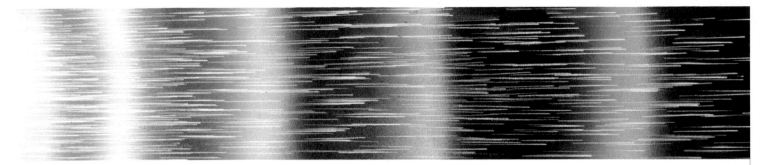

the Big Crunch?

Bang, when light began to be generated. Since then, as the universe has expanded, it has cooled a great deal.

The Big Crunch?

If it goes on growing indefinitely, the universe will become more and more empty, as the galaxies move farther and farther apart. Space will also become colder and colder. However, if the universe should at some point stop expanding and start contracting, the galaxies will no longer move away from one another but will draw together until they collide and fuse. The universe will return to its original state, a furnace of infinite density. Everything will be destroyed. This will be the **Big Crunch**.

The future of the universe depends on the average quantity of matter that it contains in a unit of volume. From

current observation, this quantity appears to be too low for the universe to cease expanding. However, if the universe proves to contain a lot of **dark matter**, there may be a limit to its expansion. ☐

The evolution of the universe

Since the Big Bang, the universe has gone on expanding and cooling. In this illustration, the universe is shown as a balloon-shaped sphere, but it may well be a different shape.

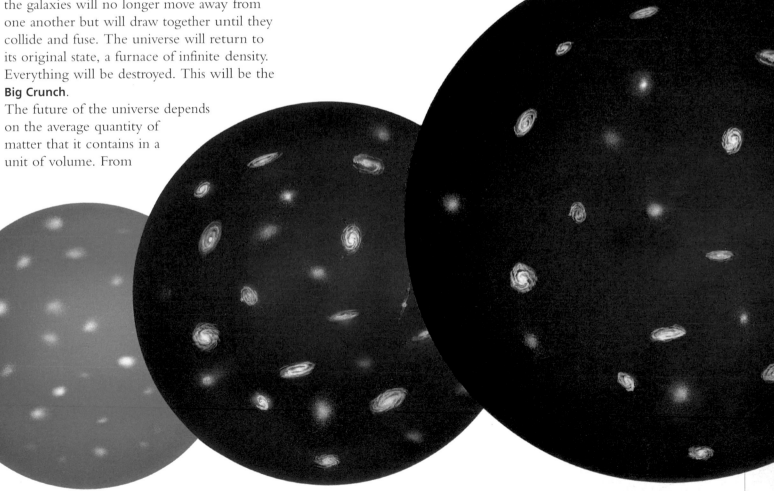

FORMATION OF GALAXIES	FORMATION OF THE SOLAR SYSTEM	THE UNIVERSE TODAY
1 billion years?	10 billion years?	15 billion years?

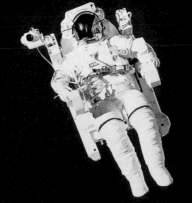

Space

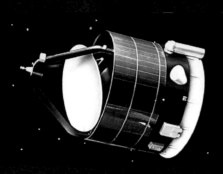

exp|oration

Launch vehicles

Launch vehicles are used to send people or equipment into space. There are two main kinds: rockets, which can be used only once, and shuttles, which are reusable spacecraft.

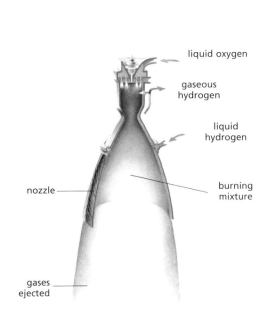

- **artificial satellite:** human-made object sent to orbit the Earth, Moon, planets or Sun.
- **booster:** rocket engine used by launch vehicles to provide enough acceleration to lift off from the ground and enter space.
- **geostationary:** describes an artificial satellite that revolves around the Earth on the plane of the equator, at about 35,800 km (22,250 miles) high. Viewed from the Earth, it appears stationary.
- **launch vehicle:** rocket capable of sending a payload into space.
- **orbiter:** spacecraft that carries out its mission while remaining in orbit around the Earth or another body.
- **payload:** the useful load carried into space, such as scientific instruments for carrying out observations.
- **probe:** unmanned spacecraft designed to study distant planets or to explore the solar system.
- **rocket:** vehicle propelled by one or more engines.
- **shuttle:** recoverable spacecraft that can fly from the ground into a low orbit around the Earth and return.
- **space capsule:** small recoverable spacecraft used to carry astronauts, animals or scientific equipment.
- **space plane:** aircraft with engines that can take it from the ground and into space.

A **launch vehicle** has two tasks. First, it must transport its load (manned craft, artificial **satellite** or deep-space **probe**) from the Earth into space. Then it must travel fast enough to put the load into orbit around the Earth or send it beyond. To do this, a launch vehicle has rocket engines.

Rocket engines

Rocket engines are thrust or jet engines that can propel a craft both through the atmosphere and through the airless vacuum of space. A rocket engine works on the principle of action and reaction—every action gives rise to an equal and opposite reaction. When a mass is ejected in one direction, the body that ejects the mass is pushed in the opposite direction.

liquid oxygen

gaseous hydrogen

liquid hydrogen

burning mixture

nozzle

gases ejected

A rocket engine. Chemical propellants are mixed and burned. Hot gases shoot out through a nozzle, sending the rocket in the opposite direction.

U.S. Saturn 5 Moon rocket

Rockets

A space **rocket** is a long metal cylinder, generally from 30 to 60 m (100–200 ft) high. On top, protected by a nose cone, is the **payload** to be carried into space. Below it are several sections or stages, usually three, each with fuel tanks and engines. Rockets take off vertically, boosted by several rocket engines. Each stage fires in sequence, and when its fuel is burned up it falls away into the atmosphere. Rockets can be used only once, and none of their parts are usually recovered. Their useful life is short, usually from 10 to 20 minutes, just long enough to put their load into orbit around the Earth.

A rocket is basically an enormous tank of propellant. In the case of the European Space Agency's Ariane rocket, for example, the

Space shuttle launch pads at Cape Canaveral, Florida

propellant makes up about 90 percent of the total mass at liftoff; the rocket structure about 9 percent; and the payload (the cargo) only 1 percent.

Nowadays a variety of rockets are in use, ranging from the small Israeli launcher Shavit, about 20 tons at launch and able to lift 160 kg (352 lbs) into orbit, to the huge Russian launcher Energia, which weighs 2,200 tons and can put a 100-ton load into orbit.

The Ariane launchers

In the 1970s, the countries of western Europe set up a joint organization, the European Space Agency, and decided to build a rocket capable of launching large satellites. The Ariane rocket has been built in several versions, each more powerful than the last. Ariane 1 appeared in 1979. Launch capacity was increased in the more powerful Ariane 2 and Ariane 3 versions. Ariane 4, in use since 1989, can launch satellites weighing from 2 to 4 tons into high **geostationary** orbits around the Earth.

The latest in the series, the Ariane 5, a new and larger design, is able to launch a satellite weighing nearly seven tons or two smaller satellites together. Ariane 5 has been used to launch modules for the International Space Station, which has been occupied since October 2000.

Ariane 5

The Ariane 5 rocket has a powerful engine burning liquid hydrogen and oxygen. On either side of the central section containing this engine are two solid-fueled boosters, each 31 m (101 ft) long and 3 m (10 ft) in diameter. Inside each booster are 240 tons of solid propellant. The total height of the rocket varies from 45 to 50 m (148–164 ft). □

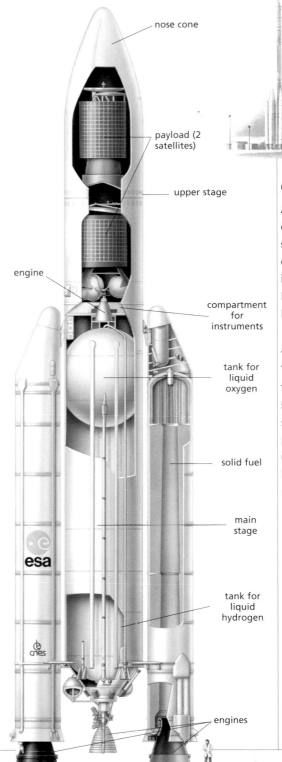

nose cone

payload (2 satellites)

upper stage

engine

compartment for instruments

tank for liquid oxygen

solid fuel

main stage

tank for liquid hydrogen

engines

Proton (Russia)

LM-4 (China)

H2 (Japan)

Other launch vehicles

Ariane is a successful launcher, especially of commercial satellites. Other rockets with comparable performance include the U.S. Atlas 2AS and Delta 2, Russia's Proton, China's Long March 4, and Japan's H2.

Ariane 5

The Ariane launcher, showing the tow boosters and the three stages that fire in sequence to send a satellite into orbit. A person is shown to scale (bottom right of diagram), illustrating the huge size of the rocket.

A Shuttle liftoff

Space shuttles and space planes

Launching the Arabsat
communications satellite from the Shuttle.

Vertical take-off

Delta Clipper
**The American Delta Clipper is
a small-scale model of a new
launcher, tested in 1993. Like a
1950s science-fiction
rocket, it has a single
reusable stage, and takes
off and lands vertically.**

Stages in a Space Shuttle mission:

1 liftoff
2 Booster rockets jettisoned
3 External fuel tank
jettisoned
4 Orbital flight (and, in
this example, release
of satellite)
5 Leaving orbit
6 Reentry
into the
atmosphere
7 Descent
through the
atmosphere
8 Landing

Rockets are a convenient method of sending
payloads into space. but they are wasteful,
since they can be used only once. A
recoverable and at least partly reusable form
of space transport was introduced by the
United States in 1981—the Space
Shuttle.

The Space Shuttle

The Shuttle is a launch vehicle
and orbital spacecraft
combined. Its major advantage
is that most of it can be used
again and again. It can travel
into space to repair a damaged
satellite or with a crew of
astronauts to a height of several
hundred kilometers. However, it cannot
operate far enough away from Earth to
launch **geostationary satellites.**
The main part of the shuttle is the orbiter,
which is given a name. Five have been
built so far: Challenger, Columbia,
Discover, Atlantis, and Endeavor.
The orbiter looks like a delta-wing
aircraft, 37 m (121 ft) long, with a
wingspan of 24 m (79 ft). At the
front of the fuselage is a split-level
pressurized cabin for the crew of
up to eight people. In the
center is a spacious cargo
bay for the payload:

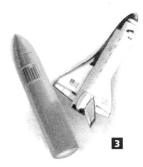

A Shuttle landing by night

satellites, space laboratories, or instrument platforms. At the rear of the orbiter are three main rocket engines used for liftoff and two other engines used for maneuvers in space. For liftoffs the orbiter needs two **booster** rockets and takes fuel from an enormous external fuel tank. This tank is not reusable. It contains the liquid hydrogen and oxygen fuel for the main engines. The Shuttle is used for missions of one to two weeks in space. It travels in orbit between 300 and 500 km (185–300 mi) above the Earth, at a speed of about 30,000 km/h (19,000 mph). When its mission is completed, the Shuttle lands like a glider on an airstrip.

Other shuttles

Russia has also built a shuttle, known as Buran (Russian for "snowstorm"). It was flown without a crew in 1988. Buran is similar to the U.S. Shuttle, but with one major difference. At takeoff, it is attached to an enormous Energia rocket. The orbiter itself has only small engines for maneuvering and directional control in space. Because of cuts in Russia's space budget, Buran now seems unlikely ever to carry people into space. Japan is developing a small unmanned shuttle, Hope. This will also be boosted into space by a rocket. European engineers carried out preliminary studies for a mini-shuttle, Hermes, that could have carried astronauts and instruments, to be launched by an Ariane 5 rocket. However, the project was abandoned as too expensive.

Space planes

The cost of launching a satellite is still very high. In the 21st century it may become cheaper, if orbital planes can be built. These craft will be entirely reusable. They will take off and land at an airport, like conventional jet planes, but their engines will be able to work in space as well as in air and will boost them into low orbits around the Earth. The space plane will need revolutionary new engines, burning oxygen while in the atmosphere and liquid oxygen when in space. It will fly at supersonic speeds, reaching 25 times the speed of sound. Building these new spacecraft poses several technical problems. They will need not only new engines, but also new materials that are light yet strong enough to withstand the very high temperatures and stresses of flight at supersonic speeds through the atmosphere. Considerable advances will be needed also in automatic flight control systems and aerodynamics.

Future propulsion systems

In the future, new ways of propulsion will be needed for voyages into deep space. At present, spacecraft have to carry vast amounts of fuel just to get into orbit. Electric motors using nuclear reactions and ejecting a beam of fast-moving atomic particles may be used. To explore the solar system craft could use solar sails (shown below). These would be large, lightweight reflective surfaces that would drift through space propelled by the particles (photons) of the Sun's light. The bigger and more reflective the sail is, the faster it is accelerated by the solar wind. With a sail, craft could make long voyages of exploration.

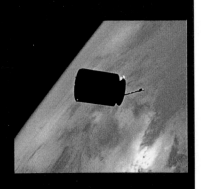

In 1957, the Soviets launched Sputnik 1, the first artificial satellite. Since then, almost 4,000 satellites have been launched for many different tasks, from observing the Earth to relaying TV programs and telephone calls.

Artificial satellites

- ◗ **artificial satellite:** object made by people, sent to orbit the Earth, Moon, planets or Sun.
- ◗ **atmosphere:** layer of gas surrounding the Earth and some other planets.
- ◗ **ellipse:** flattened circular shape described by one body as it orbits another in space.
- ◗ **geostationary:** describes an artificial satellite that revolves around the Earth on the plane of the equator, at about 35,800 km (22,250 mi) high. Viewed from the Earth, it appears stationary.
- ◗ **orbit:** closed curved path that one body describes in space around another body of greater mass.
- ◗ **period (of revolution):** time taken for one orbit by an artificial satellite.
- ◗ **planet:** a nonluminous body in space revolving around a star.
- ◗ **revolution:** movement of a planet around the Sun or of a satellite around its planet.
- ◗ **Shuttle:** recoverable spacecraft that can fly from the ground into a low orbit around the Earth and return.
- ◗ **solar system:** the Sun and its family of planets, asteroids and other bodies, and the space around them.

Artificial satellites are objects launched into space from Earth. They orbit the Earth or another body, such as the Moon, or a **planet.** They are launched by a rocket or shuttle, and are made of special materials so they can withstand the hostile space environment. Most artificial satellites have been put into **orbit** around the Earth, but satellites have also been sent to orbit the Moon, the Sun, and the planets Venus and Mars. By firing a small engine, a satellite can change its orbit. It can even move away from the Earth into space.

Surviving the dangers of space

The satellite's structure has to carry various pieces of equipment and also act as a screen to protect it from harmful radiation and bombardment by tiny meteorites. Any object in space is constantly hit by rays, particles and fragments of dust. There is no **atmosphere** to protect a spacecraft or satellite from these impacts, and since space is a vacuum, differences in temperature are extreme. A satellite facing the Sun can roast at 150°C (300°F). In shadow it freezes at −150°C (−238°F).

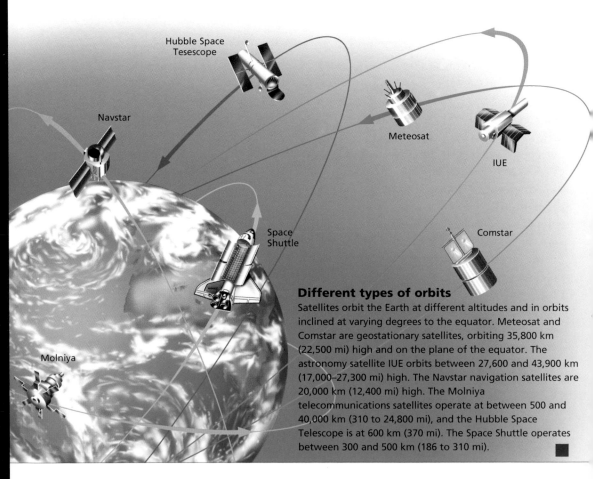

Hubble Space Telescope

Navstar

Meteosat

IUE

Space Shuttle

Comstar

Molniya

Different types of orbits

Satellites orbit the Earth at different altitudes and in orbits inclined at varying degrees to the equator. Meteosat and Comstar are geostationary satellites, orbiting 35,800 km (22,500 mi) high and on the plane of the equator. The astronomy satellite IUE orbits between 27,600 and 43,900 km (17,000–27,300 mi) high. The Navstar navigation satellites are 20,000 km (12,400 mi) high. The Molniya telecommunications satellites operate at between 500 and 40,000 km (310 to 24,800 mi), and the Hubble Space Telescope is at 600 km (370 mi). The Space Shuttle operates between 300 and 500 km (186 to 310 mi).

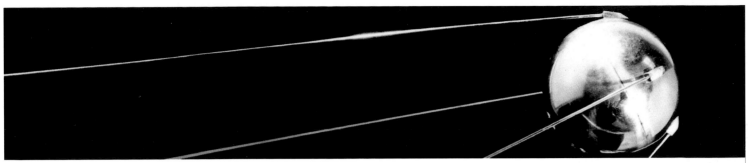

Sputnik 1, the first artificial satellite

Inside a satellite

Satellites are generally made of lightweight metals such as alloys or aluminum and titanium, and composite materials. They must be strong and long-lasting. Satellites contain many systems and mechanical parts, which must keep working automatically while the satellite is in orbit. They include equipment for opening up and directing solar panels or telecommunications antennae; temperature control equipment; power-generating units to make instruments work; equipment for correcting or changing orbit, or for stabilizing the satellite; and units to manage the data recorded on board and to keep open communications with receiving stations on the ground.

The orbits of satellites

A satellite in orbit around the Earth or another body travels in a closed path known as its **orbit**. The orbit takes the shape of an **ellipse**, or a flattened curve. The point of orbit closest to the center of the Earth is the perigee. The farthest point from the center of the Earth is the apogee. The time taken for one complete **revolution** around the Earth is the **period**.
Satellites can be placed in orbit at varying angles to the Earth. This means that they can overfly different regions of the planet. Some satellites orbit on the plane of the equator, others on the plane of the poles. Others orbit at different angles. A satellite may have an orbit as low as 1,000 km (620 mi) or, like the **geostationary** satellites, make a circular orbit on the plane of the equator at 35,800 km (22,500 mi) above the planet, staying above the same area of the surface.

Testing a satellite on the ground: this special chamber has walls that do not reflect sound waves to simulate the vacuum of space.

Geostationary satellites

Satellites that orbit on the plane of the equator, at 35,800 km (22,250 mi) above the Earth, revolve once in 23 hours 56 minutes. This is exactly the same time it takes the Earth to rotate once on its axis. Viewed from the Earth, such satellites seem to remain in the same place in the sky, hence their name "geostationary." Most telecommunications satellites are geostationary. They act as relays for telephones, television and computer links between places on the Earth that may be thousands of kilometers apart on different continents. Among the most powerful telecommunications satellites are the Intelsat 7 satellites (shown below), first launched in 1993 by the International Satellite Consortium.

A control room for space flights

How satellites are used

Fixed on the Sun

Some satellites keep a fixed position in space in relation to the Sun. These are "heliosynchronous" satellites. Many satellites used to observe the Earth, for example, the French SPOT satellites and the U.S. LANDSATs, are heliosynchronous. They pass over a particular area of the Earth always at the same solar time, and therefore always under the same conditions of sunlight.

Satellites are now indispensable tools, with many uses in telecommunications and scientific research. They also have military uses. Satellites can make observations and send high-quality information immediately to the ground. Most satellites go on working for several years, for as long as 10 to 15 years in some cases.

Uses of satellites

Three out of four satellites launched have military uses. For example, they collect data (by photography, radar and other means) about military installations and equipment and even monitor troop movements. The remaining satellites are those with civil and commercial uses, or for scientific research. Telecommunications satellites have given us instantaneous communications between the continents, and major world events can be seen on live television in all parts of the world. Direct-broadcasting satellites beam TV programs to homes fitted with "satellite dishes." Special satellites survey the Earth's weather systems, aiding weather forecasters. Other satellites map the Earth's resources (such as water, vegetation and minerals). Satellites can help ships to navigate, observe floods, droughts and pollution, and even track migrating animals. Astronomical satellites scan the universe for new stars or other unknown phenomena in deep space.

The ERS 1 satellite

This radar image, coded in different colors, shows the Camargue region and the Cevennes mountains in France. It was obtained in 1992 from the European satellite ERS 1 (shown above).

On this computer-generated image, each point represents a space object orbiting the Earth.

A satellite in space

Transmitting information

All exchanges of information between a satellite and the ground are by radio. Satellites have radio antennae for sending and receiving radio signals. Space agencies use networks of ground stations to communicate with satellites throughout their orbits. Signals sent to a satellite tell it to do something—for example, to switch on an engine or to deploy an antenna. Satellites send signals back to Earth to transmit the results of their observations and instrument readings. This is known as telemetry. Special radio frequencies are used to ensure uninterrupted communications.

Space debris

Ever since we began to send rockets into space, leftovers have been piling up in space around the Earth. This debris includes disused satellites, the upper stages of rockets, fragments of rockets that exploded, and all kinds of odd pieces of equipment jettisoned into space after use.

A section of the U.S. Department of Defense has a network of radar scanners and telescope cameras to survey "space junk" and keep track of satellites still operating. The section's headquarters are beneath a mountain in Colorado. About 7,000 objects larger than 10 cm (4 in) across are permanently monitored, a number that includes only 400 operational satellites.

In addition, there are between 30,000 and 70,000 pieces of smaller debris, too small to be detected from the ground. Such debris represents a potential hazard to satellites and to astronanuts making space walks. Their high speed makes them formidable missiles, capable of puncturing an astronaut's spacesuit or of damaging a spaceship. At a speed of 10 km/s (30 ft/s), a grain of dust measuring

A radar image of the south of France taken from space

only 3 mm (a quarter inch) has the same destructive force as a ball bowled at 100 km/h (62 mph). Debris reenters the atmosphere on average of once a week. Usually it breaks up completely in the atmosphere. Occasionally, when the objects are very large or are radioactive, falling fragments present a danger to people. This was the case during the uncontrolled reentry into the atmosphere of the U.S. Skylab laboratory over Australia in July 1979 and of the Russian orbital station Salyut 7 over South America in February 1991. However, no one has yet been killed by falling space debris. ☐

A satellite for sale

Objects that have traveled in space are now collector's items. Part of the Russian Photon satellite was recovered after two weeks in orbit around the Earth in 1990. Weighing over two tons, it was sold at auction in Paris in 1992.

A space dustbin

In the future, growing amounts of space debris around the Earth could become dangerous for satellites and astronauts. There are already plans to send satellite rubbish collectors into space to gather up debris, before it reenters the atmosphere and burns up.

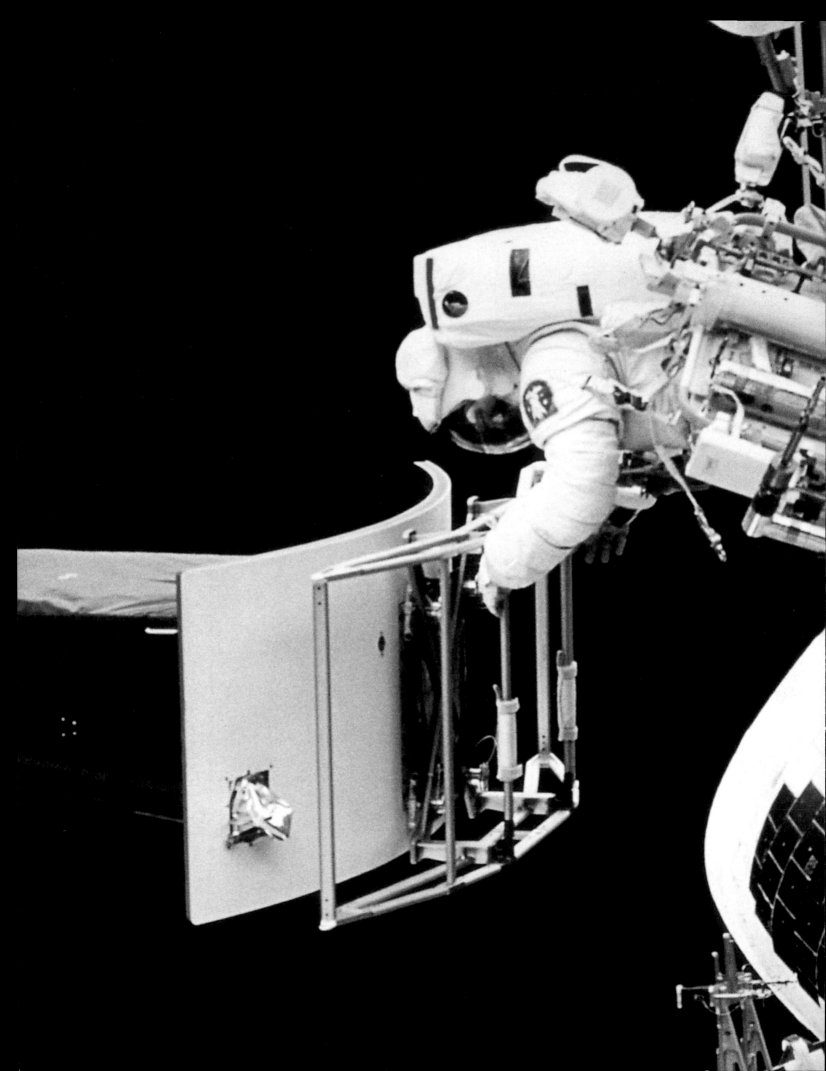

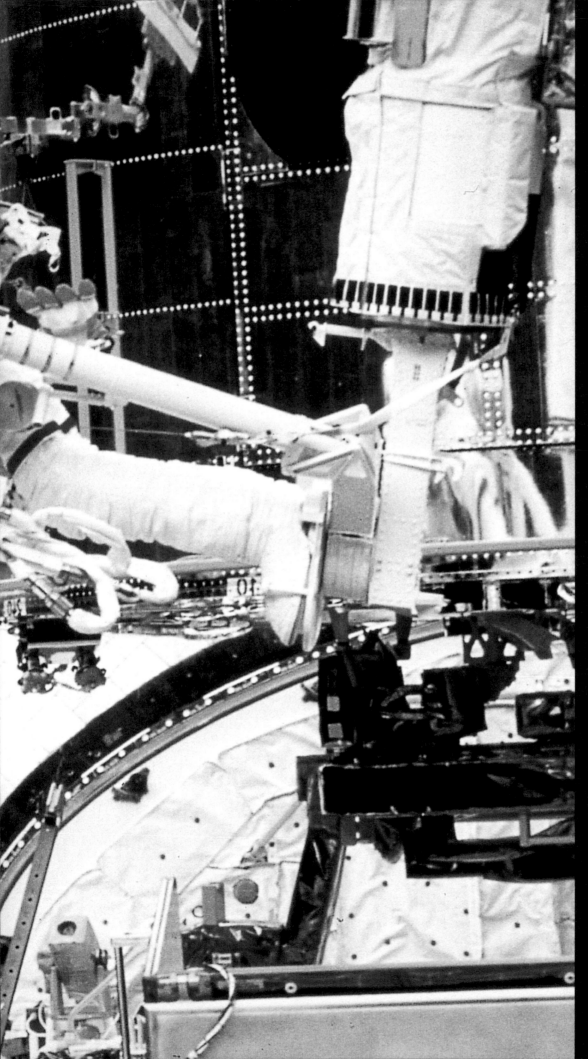

Repairing the Hubble Telescope

The Hubble Space Telescope suffered from both "near-sightedness" and tremors. In December 1993, a U.S. Space Shuttle crew went to recover and repair it. Five spacewalks, amounting to 36 hours of work in space, were needed to complete the operation successfully. The telescope was handicapped by a defect in the shape of its main mirror and by vibrations. Close to the large mirror the astronauts fitted corrective lenses. These were designed to sharpen the images of the stars under observation.

Space probes travel across the solar system to study planets, comets and asteroids. Several dozen probes, each equipped with instruments including cameras, have so far left the Earth.

Space probes

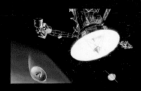

Space probes are special satellites. They are designed to be put into orbit around the Sun or to make long voyages in space to reach the body they are to study. A space probe's **mission** is complex and costly. To rendezvous with a planet at a great distance from the Earth requires much preparation. The probe must be launched at a precise time (calculated from the positions of the Earth and of the target body). The journey takes from four to six months to reach Venus, nearly a year to Mars, and several years to Jupiter and the farther planets. Since the probe will not usually return to Earth, its instruments must be able to work for a long time in space without breaking down and be able to transmit by radio all the information the probe collects.

How is a planet targeted?

To reach a **planet**, a probe does not simply follow a straight line. Since all the planets (except Mercury and Pluto) **orbit** in approximately the same plane, the least costly path (in fuel use) is an **ellipse** at a tangent to the Earth's orbit at the time of the probe's launch and also to the orbit of the target. This path is named Hohmann's trajectory, after the German engineer who was the first to calculate it. Unfortunately, although this path is the most economical, it is also the longest. A trip to Mercury would take three-and-a-half months, a journey to Pluto over 45 years! Because the planets are constantly moving, to follow Hohmann's trajectory

a probe must be launched at a very precise date. This date occurs only once every four months for Mercury, once every 19 months for Venus and once every 26 months for Mars. For a faster journey, the probe must be launched on a path that cuts across the orbits of the Earth and the target. Launching at a higher speed, a probe can be sent on such a course to Mars or Venus in only a few weeks.

Orbit and trajectory

Before a probe is sent to a planet, it is first put in a parking orbit around the Earth. The

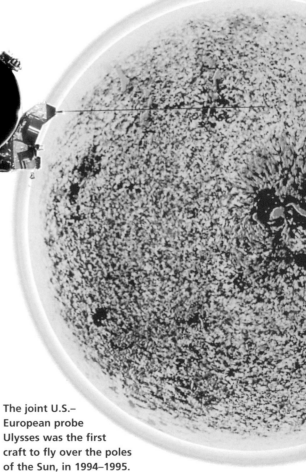

The joint U.S.–European probe Ulysses was the first craft to fly over the poles of the Sun, in 1994–1995.

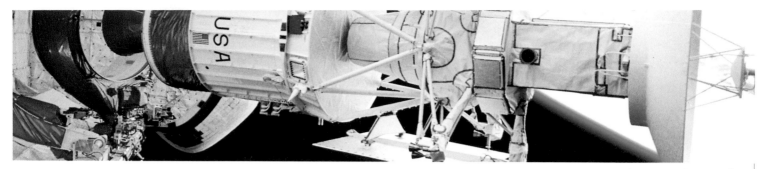

The U.S. probe Magellan

launch team then works out the precise time for the departure to the target. After several revolutions in parking orbit, the probe's rocket engine is fired to send it on its way. Even though this technique is very precise, it is often necessary to make course corrections during the flight. Once near the planet (which may take months or even years), the probe has to slow down to go into orbit. As it slows, it is captured by the planet's gravitational pull and becomes an orbital satellite.

Detecting and measuring

On board a probe are various counters, gauges and detectors. These instruments study the particles, radiation and meteorites encountered on its journey through space. Probes sent especially to study a particular planet or comet have one or more cameras, devices for detecting and analyzing the atmosphere, and instruments to measure temperature, pressure and magnetic fields.

Overflying a planet provides information about its atmosphere—how thick it is, how dense, and so on. From its orbit above a planet, the probe can take the same readings many times as it passes over the surface. If the probe is designed to land instruments on the planet, it can study the chemistry and geology and check for physical and quake activity. Analysis of the trajectory of the probe is also useful, since it gives scientists more information about the planet's mass and the strength of the gravity on its surface. ☐

In 2004 the European probe Huygens will study the atmosphere of Titan, Saturn's largest moon, and will land on its surface.

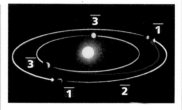

Hohmann's trajectory

To send a spacecraft to Mars (1) using the least energy, it must be fired on a trajectory in the form of an ellipse (2), at a tangent to both the Earth's orbit (3) at the time of launch and to Mars' orbit at the time of arrival. Such a voyage takes more than a year.

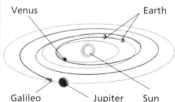

A "gravity assist"

When a probe flies past a planet, the gravitational attraction exercised on it by the planet can be used to curve its trajectory, increase its speed, and "hurl" it away toward another planet. Using this technique made it possible for the Voyager 2 probe to fly past Jupiter, Saturn, Uranus and Neptune.

The Huygens (left) and Cassini (right) space probes

Exploring the solar system

A balloon on Mars

In the next 5 to 10 years, a Russian probe will transport a French balloon to Mars. Loaded with sensors, the balloon will be released in the Martian atmosphere to drift for several days, at various altitudes. At night it will come quite close to the ground and trail a cable, also containing sensors, to collect more data.

Space flight has been our first step toward breaking our link to the Earth. For the foreseeable future, our exploring will be confined to the solar system. The distances are immense, and with current spacecraft, a voyage to leave the solar system would last for hundreds of years. Exploration of the solar system began with the Moon, the body closest to Earth. Then probes were sent to study the distant planets.

Exploring the Moon

From 1959, only two years after the launch of the first artificial satellite, the Soviet Union began to send unmanned probes to the Moon. Luna 3 sent back the first photographs of the Moon's hidden side. Throughout the 1960s the race to explore the Moon spurred the Americans and Soviets into com- petition. The U.S. launched the Lunar Orbiter probes, which orbited the Moon as satellites and allowed favorable sites for a

landing by astronauts to be chosen. In 1966, the Soviets were the first to make a soft landing on the Moon, with the Luna 9 probe, and they also sent Luna 10 into orbit around the Moon.

Between 1969 and 1972 the United States carried off the main prize, with the manned Apollo flights to the Moon. On 22 July 1969 Neil Armstrong and Edwin Aldrin of the Apollo 11 mission were the first people to walk on the Moon. Twelve astronauts in all landed on the Moon, at six different places. They took thousands of photographs and set up scientific instruments.

Although the Soviets did not send people to the Moon, they went on exploring with unmanned lunar probes until 1976. In 1971 and 1973 Soviet probes landed robot vehicles, known as Lunokhods, on the Moon.

In the future, robots will allow thorough exploration of the surface of Mars.

The European space probe Giotto

Exploring the planets

The flyby mission to Venus of the U.S. Mariner 2 probe on 14 December 1962 marked the beginning of the exploration of the planets. Other flights followed, of which these are the most notable.

First flyby mission

Venus: 1962, Mariner 2 (USA)
Mars: 1965, Mariner 4 (USA)
Jupiter: 1973, Pioneer 10 (USA)
Mercury: 1974, Mariner 10 (USA)
Saturn: 1979, Pioneer 11 (USA)
Uranus: 1986, Voyager 2 (USA)
Neptune: 1989, Voyager 2 (USA)

First orbiting

Venus: 1975, Venera 9 and Venera 10 (USSR)
Mars: 1971, Mariner 9 (USA)

First landing

Venus: 1967, Venera 4 (USSR)
Mars: 1971, Mars 3 (USSR)

In less than 30 years, all the planets apart from Pluto have been flown past. Spacecraft have orbited Venus and Mars, and landing probes have been set down on these two planets. NASA's Mars Global Surveyor satellite, which has orbited the red planet since 1997, found gullies and other traces of erosion, probably formed by running water. The discovery sparked hopes that life may exist on Mars.

The two Voyager probes, launched in 1977, provided a wealth of photographs and scientific information on four giant planets— Jupiter, Saturn, Uranus and Neptune—and on their rings and satellites. From 1990 to 1994, the U.S. Magellan probe stayed in orbit around Venus and mapped the surface through the thick clouds of the planet's atmosphere using radar. The U.S. Cassini probe toward Saturn was launched 15 October 1997. It carries the European Huygens probe, which will land on Saturn's largest moon, Titan. The two spacecraft will not arrive at their destination until 2004.

Comet and asteroid flybys

Exploration of the solar system includes studying asteroids and comets. In 1985, the American ICE probe approached the Giacobini-Zinner comet and crossed its tail. In 1986, two Japanese probes, two Soviet probes and one European probe flew past Halley's comet. The European probe, Giotto, passed only 600 km (370 miles) from the comet's nucleus and took the first photographs of the nucleus of a comet. Exploration of asteroids began with the flybys of Gaspra (1991) and Ida (1993) by the U.S. Galileo probe on its way to Jupiter.

Interplanetary space

Interplanetary space contains dust and atomic particles. Specific probes, including the first Pioneers, have studied them, discovering the existence of **solar wind** and the **magnetosphere** that surrounds some planets, including the Earth. Other probes have been sent out to observe the Sun. The Ulysses probe, launched in 1990 as part of a joint U.S.–European study, was the first to overfly the poles of the Sun, which are very hard to observe from the Earth. ☐

Moon photographed by Clementine

During two months in 1994, a small U.S. military probe, Clementine, transmitted more than a million photographs of the Moon: a complete lunar atlas. For the first time, detailed pictures were obtained of the polar regions.

A sample of lunar rock seen though a microscope

Astronauts brought back more than 380 kg (840 lbs) of moon rocks, which have undergone all kinds of tests in laboratories. Lunar rock is a lot less varied than Earth rock. There are two main types: anorthosites, which are very abundant in the mountains, and basalts, which fill the maria or "seas." Both are igneous (volcanic) rocks.

The first person to fly in space was the Soviet cosmonaut Yuri Gagarin, on 12 April 1961. He orbited the Earth in 1 hour 48 minutes on board Vostok 1. Since then, more than 300 astronauts have traveled in space.

People in space

- **cabin:** part of spacecraft reserved for the crew.
- **centrifuge:** rotating machine designed to simulate the feeling of acceleration.

- **gravity:** force acting on objects on a planet or in its vicinity; it gives bodies their "weight" and tends to make them fall toward the planet, or to be held in orbit around it.
- **orbital station:** large spacecraft, unmanned or manned, orbiting the Earth, usually designed for long missions.
- **parabolic flight:** flight path by an airplane in free fall, which achieves for a few seconds inside its fuselage extremely low gravity, simulating the weightlessness of space.
- **pressurized:** describes an enclosure, such as a spacecraft cabin, in which atmospheric pressure is maintained at a safe level for human beings.
- **spacecraft:** space vehicle carrying scientific instruments and/or astronauts.
- **weightlessness:** absence of the effects of gravity.

The men and women selected to take part in spaceflight are known as cosmonauts in Russia and as astronauts in the United States. Nine out of ten space travelers to date have been either Russians or Americans. Others have come from 20 countries.

Becoming an astronaut

Selection of astronauts is rigorous, and candidates must pass a series of tests. They must be in excellent physical condition, with very good sight and hearing, mentally well-balanced, and with a scientific or technical education. The first American astronauts chosen for the 1960s flights were all less than 40 years old, with advanced degrees in engineering, and trained as test pilots with at least 1,500 hours' flying time.

Training

Intensive training prepares men and women for life in space. Astronauts study the theory of spaceflight. They do various exercises in conditions that reproduce some characteristics of space travel. These include simulations in a **centrifuge** of the severe acceleration stresses they experience at liftoff; simulation inside an airplane flying a **parabolic flight** path of the **weightlessness** they will experience in orbit; and simulation in a water tank of working in a spacesuit in space. Training of space crews in Russia takes

French astronauts training for a mission on board the Russian Mir space station

Cosmonauts ready to board their spacecraft

about two years. The different phases of the flight are practiced painstakingly in flight simulators. The simulator is an exact reproduction of the spacecraft **cabin**. Each member of the crew must be able to take over the job of a colleague in case of sickness. In the United States, there are two types of astronaut. Pilots and mission specialists are trained to take control of the spacecraft. Payload specialists are engineers or scientists, trained for three months only in the safety aspects of the flight. Their job is to carry out scientific and engineering experiments.

Astronauts practice underwater the work they will do during a spacewalk.

Life support

An astronaut wears a spacesuit for protection and to keep him or her alive in space. The suit supplies oxygen for breathing and helps the body withstand acceleration forces. Spacesuits are **pressurized** so astronauts can go out into the vacuum of space.

In the first manned spacecraft, astronauts wore suits all the time. Nowadays, the cabins of spacecraft are thought safe enough for people to work inside them without special clothing. Astronauts wear spacesuits only from liftoff until the craft enters orbit and during reentry into the atmosphere. They also wear suits when leaving the craft to work outside.

Space sickness

Life in a spacecraft in orbit is altered by **weightlessness**. Without **gravity**, astronauts cannot walk. They and objects around them float, and top and bottom have no meaning. Most astronauts suffer dizzy spells or vomiting during the first day in space. This "space sickness" vanishes as the body gets used to being in space. However, weightlessness causes significant changes to the heart and blood vessels, bones, muscles and sense of balance. Blood tends to rise to the upper part of the body, which makes the face swollen. Bones lose calcium, muscles become weaker, and the skeleton gets longer. When they return to Earth after a long mission, astronauts must readapt to gravity, and for some time they have problems with balance and coordination. ☐

A spacewalk

Everyday life in space

The astronauts who went to the Moon spent just over a week in space. The missions of the Shuttle can last up to two weeks. The longest stays in space take place on board **orbital space stations** that can remain in orbit around the Earth for years. The station is made up of sections or modules, which are launched separately and assembled in space. The Russian Mir station, for example, was used until 1997. Cosmonauts visited it in relays, so that they could complete lengthy scientific and medical experiments. One man spent 437 days in Mir, returning to Earth in March 1995.

Eating in space

Astronauts eat canned foods, and also chilled and freeze-dried foods. Liquids must be kept sealed, or else they would disperse as droplets because of the lack of gravity. Drinks are kept in plastic sacs and sucked through tubes.

Sleeping in space

To go to bed, an astronaut slides inside a sleeping bag attached to the spacecraft wall. Sleep can be difficult inside a cramped craft that is never dark and rarely silent.

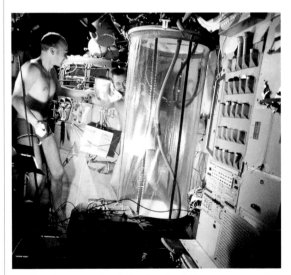

The shower unit of the Soviet Salyut space station

Personal hygiene

In space, astronauts wash just as they would on Earth, but with certain modifications. They use moist towels or take specially designed showers (water must not escape to float around the cabin). Razors have a compartment to collect stubble for the same reason. Space toilets suck in waste and eject it into space.

Work and leisure

During the day, astronauts have a full work program. They carry out scientific and technical experiments. The main difficulty in working while weightless is that it is impossible to put anything down without securing it. So there are straps and Velcro strips along the walls and worktops of the spacecraft. To keep themselves in place at their work, astronauts keep their legs and feet in special restraints.

When not working, they relax by reading, listening to music and watching TV. Cosmonauts aboard the Mir station regularly talked with their families by radio, while Progress space transports ferried up letters and videos of news and current events. Astronauts must keep fit and regularly exercise on running machines and exercise bikes. Mir cosmonauts did a two-hour workout every day to keep their muscles in condition.

Spacewalks

On 18 March 1965, Alekseï Leonov, copilot of the Soviet spacecraft Voshod 2, became the first spacewalker. Protected by his spacesuit and attached to the craft by a lifeline, he maneuvered for 12 minutes outside in space. Since then spacewalks or EVAs (extra-vehicular activities) have become commonplace and may last several hours. Astronauts leave the spacecraft to do repairs, such as freeing a jammed antenna or reloading a TV camera, or even to retrieve a satellite. The first spacewalks showed that astronauts had difficulty moving precisely in space. They needed holds to cling to as well

An astronaut at work outside the Space Shuttle

as specially adapted tools. They also tired quickly. Modern craft have handholds around the outside to help astronauts move about and keep in one position while working. One of the most dramatic spacewalks took place in December 1993. Shuttle astronauts successfully recovered the Hubble Space Telescope and brought it into the Endeavor orbiter. There it was repaired before being released again into space. Four astronauts worked in pairs, making five spacewalks lasting 35 hours 28 minutes in all. Spacewalks will be indispensable for assembling parts of future space stations orbiting the Earth. □

Inside the Mir space station

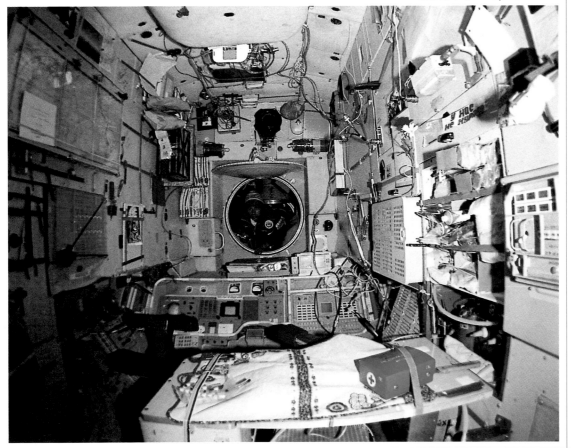

The Challenger disaster

On 28 January 1986, the twenty-fifth Shuttle mission ended in disaster seventy seconds after liftoff. The Shuttle exploded in flight, killing all seven astronauts aboard. The accident was caused by the rupture of a joint seal on one of the two booster rockets. A spurt of burning gas escaped through the crack, then the rocket split in two. Flames entered the main external fuel tank, filled with liquid oxygen and hydrogen, which exploded, consuming the orbiter.

The future

The goal of space flights in the dawn of the 21st century will be to assemble an international space station. Scientists also hope to continue the exploration of the Moon.

- **gravity:** force acting on objects on a planet or in its vicinity; it gives bodies their weight and tends to make them fall toward the planet, or to be held in orbit around it.
- **module:** part of a spacecraft, usually a self-contained unit with a particular function.
- **pressurized:** describes an enclosure, such as a spacecraft cabin, in which atmospheric pressure is maintained at a safe level for human beings.
- **radio telescope:** instrument designed to collect, detect and analyze radio waves emitted by the stars.
- **shuttle:** recoverable spacecraft that can fly from the ground into a low orbit around the Earth and return.
- **solar panel:** array of photovoltaic cells that transform light energy from

the Sun into electrical energy.
- **space station:** an orbital space laboratory in which crews can live and work for as long as a year in space.

The costs of large space programs are so high that no single country can afford them alone. The achievements of the future will come through international cooperation and shared knowledge.

The international space station

The U.S. decided to build an orbital **space station** in 1984. However, the 1986 Challenger disaster delayed the project, and rising costs made the U.S. space agency NASA invite foreign partners to join. Canada, Europe, Japan, and Russia (which has long experience of space stations through the Salyut and Mir programs) agreed to take part.

A series of joint Russian and American manned flights gathered data for the development of the station. The heart of the station is the Russian-made Zvezda **module**, which provides the astronauts with beds, indoor plumbing, propulsion, and power capabilities. In July 2000, Zvezda docked with Zarya, the Russian cargo module, and Unity, the U.S.-made connecting node, which had been orbiting since 1998. In 2001, crews will install solar panels, an airlock, and a laboratory module. The

Drawing of proposed lunar radio telescopes

International Space Station will have roughly the same volume as a three-bedroom house. Scientists plan to use the ISS for research into biotechnology, engineering, and studies of Earth from space. The space station could also be used as a launchpad for longer explorations within the solar system.

Return to the Moon

It is an astronomer's dream to put telescopes and **radio telescopes** on the Moon. Its far side would be an ideal site to observe outer space. On the Moon, there is no atmosphere to blur images, no interference from city lights or pollution, and a lunar night lasting two weeks. The Moon could become a natural space station. Scientists could use it to study how astronauts react to long periods of living in weak gravity and exposed to the full force of radiation. The next program of Moon exploration will

probably be international and will involve sending unmanned craft.

Some of these will stay in orbit to photograph and study the Moon. Others will land mobile robots to explore specific regions and analyze the lunar soil. Probes will retrieve soil samples and bring them back to Earth. The final step will be to build a scientific base on the Moon, to which astronauts will travel for periodic visits.

Lunar bases

Plans for lunar bases already exist. The living quarters will be **pressurized**. To protect the occupants from the dangerous radiation originating in space and from the meteorites that bombard the Moon constantly, it will be partly buried beneath the rocky material of the Moon's surface. Huge **solar panels** will convert sunlight into electricity, which will be stored for use during the long lunar nights. Oxygen will be extracted from the lunar rocks, in which it is abundant. At such a lunar base, astronauts will learn to live and work in a world beyond the Earth. They will need this experience if we hope to venture farther across the solar system, for example, to explore Mars. ▫

The International Space Station
Once assembled, the station was propelled by its own engines to an altitude of 440 km (273 mi), where it orbits. Teams of six astronauts will work on board, and the space station should operate for ten years. ■

European shuttle

The international space station of the future may be served by a small European-built shuttle craft. The CTV or Crew Transport Vehicle will carry into orbit four spacesuited astronauts and 1.5 tons of cargo.

Colonization of space

U.S. physicist Gerard O'Neill has predicted that in the future people will build "space cities." These space colonies will look like huge wheels, spinning slowly to create their own artificial gravity. Thousands of people could live in them.

?

Did You Know?

Which is the hottest planet?

The hottest planet is Venus, where the temperature at ground level reaches 860°F (460°C). Venus revolves close to the Sun and is encircled by a thick atmosphere made up mainly of carbon dioxide, which holds in the heat from sunlight.

Which planet has more moons than any other?

Saturn has eighteen moons in orbit around it. Earth and Pluto each have only one moon. Of the nine planets, only Venus and Mercury have no moons.

What is our Moon's origin?

Relying on data gathered by the Apollo missions, astronomers now think that the Moon was the product of a collision between the Earth and a smaller body (about the size of Mars) that hit the Earth not long after its own formation. The fragments from that collision scattered into rings around the Earth. Later, some of the fragments combined again to give birth to the Moon.

How much does the largest meteorite ever found on the Earth weigh?

The Hoba meteorite weighs in at about sixty-six tons. It was found in 1920 on a farm about ten miles from the town of Grootfontein in Namibia, but it had fallen several centuries before. It is made of iron.

How much time does it take for light to leave the Sun?

If they did not meet any obstacles on their way, the particles of light (called photons) would only need two seconds to cross the distance from the center of the Sun, where they are emitted, to its surface. In fact, because they are constantly bumping into atoms of gas present in the Sun's interior, they take millions of years to leave the Sun. Once they have done so, they reach the Earth in only eight minutes.

How long does it take for the Sun to make a complete revolution of the Galaxy?

The Sun orbits the center of the Galaxy at a speed of about 550,000 miles an hour (900,000 km/h). It takes about 240

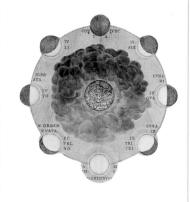

million years, then, for the Sun to go completely around the Galaxy. Since the Sun was formed, it has made about twenty of these revolutions.

Which star is closest to our solar system?

The nearest star to the solar system is Proxima Centauri. Its light takes four years and three months to reach us. With our current means of space travel, it would take about 100,000 years to get there. In a car going 100 miles an hour, the trip would last 45 million years.

What is the largest star that we know of?

A star in the constellation Auriga, the Charioteer, called E (epsilon) Aurigae, is a red super giant 2,700 times the size of the Sun, which gives it a volume 20 billion times as large as the Sun. If it were placed where the Sun is, it would engulf all of the planets as far as Saturn.

Which star will be the pole star in 12,000 years?

Right now, the pole star is the brightest star in the constellation called Ursa Minor (the Little Bear or the Little Dipper). In 12,000 years, the pole star will be Vega, the brightest star in the constellation Lyra.

Who was the first passenger on a flight that orbited the Earth?

The little dog Laika was the passenger aboard the first space flight with a live occupant, Sputnik 2, a Russian space capsule launched in 1957. She remained in orbit around the Earth for a week. When the capsule's reserves of oxygen ran out, Laika died. The capsule disintegrated as it reentered the atmosphere in April 1958. This experiment showed that a living organism could withstand being placed in orbit as well as a period of weightlessness.

What was the first active communications satellite launched into space?

The U.S. satellite Telstar 1 was launched on July 10, 1962. It was able to transmit 2.5 watts. Satellites now in use are much more powerful: Telecom 2, for example, launched by the European Space Agency in 1991, has the power to transmit 2,475 watts.

What was the first space station?

The U.S. space laboratory Skylab was placed in orbit in 1973. Three separate crews were brought up to the station by Apollo spacecraft. The last crew stayed there for eighty-four days in 1974. In 1979,

Skylab broke into pieces as it reentered the atmosphere, and some of its fragments fell into the Indian Ocean.

What equipment holds the record for speed in space?

The space probe Ulysses was launched by the U.S. space shuttle in 1990 toward Jupiter, which propelled it back to fly over the poles of the Sun. Ulysses traveled at speeds of more than 100,000 miles an hour (160,000 km/h)—twenty-eight miles a second.

Which satellite was the first to be repaired in orbit?

A U.S. satellite launched in 1980, the Solar Maximum Mission (SMM), nicknamed Solar Max, broke down nine months later. Astronauts were sent to repair it in place in April 1984.

Who has made the longest flight in space?

The Russian cosmonaut, Vladimir Poliakov, returned to Earth on March 26, 1995, after spending 442 days in orbit around the Earth.

Have messages meant for extraterrestrial life been sent into space?

In 1974, a radio message was broadcast in the direction of a cluster of stars in the

constellation Hercules. This message will reach its destination in about 25,000 years (and the answer, if there is one, will come back in about 50,000 years). In 1977, a recording on videodisk was placed into two Voyager probes sent by the United States. This message from the Earth to extraterrestrials contains greetings in fifty-four languages, samples of music from different times and countries as well as sounds typical of our planet, ranging from the noise of an avalanche to the song of whales. It also includes photographs showing our planet and its inhabitants.

Do UFOs exist?

Once called flying saucers, UFOs (unidentified flying objects) are bright, fleeting objects or visual displays seen in the sky for which we have no explanation. The first sighting, in 1947, was by an American pilot who, while flying, observed nine luminous disklike shapes moving across the sky. Later, other sightings were reported. There are several organizations devoted to ufology (the study of UFOs). Nevertheless, most scientists think that UFOs are not extraterrestrial spacecraft.

Copernicus

Tycho Brahe

Galileo

Kepler

Famous People

◑ Antiquity

Hipparchus
(2nd century B.C.)

The greatest Greek astronomer of ancient times, Hipparchus listed the locations of 1,025 stars in a catalogue, in which he was the first to group stars into classes by the "magnitude" of their apparent brightness in the sky. Hipparchus also discovered the precession of the equinoxes.

Claudius Ptolemy
(2nd century B.C.)

A Greek astronomer, geographer, and mathematician, Ptolemy thought that the Earth was fixed at the center of the universe and proposed a theory relying on a combination of circular movements to account for the motions of the Sun, the Moon, and the planets in the sky.

◑ 1400s–1500s

Nicholas Copernicus
(1473–1543)

A Polish astronomer, Copernicus suggested after long years of research that the Earth and the other planets rotate on their axes and revolve around the Sun. Because it denied the Earth its privileged place in the universe, this idea sparked much criticism, notably within the Roman Catholic Church.

Tycho Brahe
(1546-1601)

Tycho, a Danish astronomer, made the most accurate observations of the heavens before the invention of the telescope. His observations of the planet Mars allowed his assistant and student, Johannes Kepler, to discover the laws of the movement of the planets around the Sun.

◑ 1600s–1800s

Galileo Galilei
(1564–1642)

In 1609-1610, Galileo, an Italian physicist and astronomer, was the first to observe the sky with a telescope, which led to his discovery of the surface of the Moon, the phases of Venus, the four main moons of Jupiter, and a multitude of stars in the Milky Way that had not been suspected till then. An advocate of the Copernican view of the universe, Galileo was tried before a tribunal of the Inquisition of the Catholic Church, which forced him to admit that he was wrong. In 1992, he was rehabilitated by the Catholic Church.

Johannes Kepler
(1571–1630)

A German astronomer and advocate of the Copernican system, Kepler discovered (using the observations made by his teacher, Tycho) the laws governing the movements of the planets around the Sun, which are still called Kepler's laws.

Isaac Newton
(1642–1727)

An English physicist, mathematician, and astronomer, Newton built the first reflecting telescope in 1671. In 1687, he stated the law of universal gravitation, which explained the movement of the planets around the Sun and of the Moon around the Earth.

William Herschel
(1738–1822)

A British astronomer, Herschel built many telescopes and discovered the planet Uranus in 1781, two of its moons in 1787, and two of the moons of Saturn in 1789. As he studied how the stars were distributed in the different parts of the sky, he discovered that the Sun is inside a flattened cluster of stars, the Galaxy.

Pierre-Simon de Laplace
(1749–1827)

Laplace, a French astronomer, mathematician, and physicist, developed the theory, still considered valid, that the solar system evolved from a cloud of interstellar gas and dust—a nebula—that began slowly to rotate.

Urbain Le Verrier
(1811–1877)

By studying the irregularities in the movement of Uranus, this French astronomer showed that another planet existed even farther away, whose orbit and position he calculated. Le Verrier thus prepared the way for the discovery of Neptune by the German astronomer Johann Galle in 1846. He was also the first to organize the publication of weather reports in France and in Europe.

◑ 1900s

Ejnar Hertzsprung
(1873–1967)

A Danish astronomer, he discovered that a relationship exists between the luminosity of stars and their surface temperatures, which can be worked out based on their spectra.

Henry Norris Russell
(1877–1957)

In 1913, Russell, an American astronomer, published a diagram in which the stars were classed by their spectra and their luminosities. It showed that there are two distinct kinds of stars—stars on the main sequence and giants. The same discovery had been made a few years before by Ejnar Hertzsprung. The Hertzsprung-Russell diagram is an indispensable tool for studying the stars.

Einstein

Goddard

Armstrong

Gagarin

Albert Einstein
(1879–1955)

A German physicist who became a U.S. citizen in 1940, Einstein was the author of the theory of relativity (1905 and 1916), which revolutionized physics and astronomy. He received the Nobel Prize for physics in 1921.

Robert Goddard
(1882–1945)

An American engineer and physicist, he was one of the pioneers of rocketry. On March 16, 1926, he launched the first liquid-fuel rocket. It flew for 2.5 seconds to a height of 40 feet.

Edwin Hubble
(1889–1953)

In 1923-24, U.S. astronomer Hubble established that galaxies existed outside our own. Then he showed that galaxies were traveling away from one another at a speed proportional to their distance (1929).

Georges Lemaître
(1894–1966)

A Belgian astronomer and mathematician, he was the first to envisage, in 1927, that the universe might be expanding. In 1931, he put forward a hypothesis of a "primeval atom." According to his hypothesis, the current universe is the product of an explosion of an enormous quantity of matter that had originally been concentrated into a very small volume. This hypothesis is the forerunner of the modern theory of the Big Bang.

Sergei Korolev
(1906–1966)

A Soviet engineer, Korolev began research into jet propulsion in 1931. He developed the Zemiorka rocket, which allowed the first artificial Earth satellite to be placed in orbit on October 4, 1957. Korolev then became the main designer of booster rockets for the U.S.S.R. His rocket, constantly improved, spearheaded the Soviet space program. More than a thousand of them were launched in various models. It is the most commonly used rocket in the world.

Valentin Glushko
(1908–1989)

A Soviet engineer, he began research in 1929 into rocket engines. Promoted to lead designer of the rocket engines for long-range Soviet ballistic missiles in 1946, he later became one of the main architects of the development of booster rockets for the U.S.S.R.

Wernher von Braun
(1912–1977)

A German engineer, he worked on the development of experimental rockets from 1930. After the German surrender in World War II, he became a U.S. citizen and one of the main architects of the U.S. space program. He oversaw the construction of the Saturn 5 rocket, which was used for launching Apollo spacecraft to the Moon.

Alan Shepard
(1923–1998)

American astronaut Shepard was the first man launched into space by the United States on May 5, 1961. Leaving Cape Canaveral, the Mercury Freedom 7 capsule that he was riding in reached an altitude of 117 miles (187 km) then fell into the Atlantic Ocean. In 1971, he served as commander of the lunar exploration mission Apollo 14.

Edwin Aldrin
(born 1930)

An American astronaut, Aldrin completed fifty-nine orbits of the Earth in 1966 as well as spacewalks. In 1969, he returned to space in the Apollo 11 mission. He was the pilot of the lunar module and the second man, after Neil Armstrong, to set foot on the Moon on July 20, 1969.

Neil Alden Armstrong
(born 1930)

American astronaut Armstrong was the commander in 1966 of the Gemini 8 mission, in which docking of two spacecraft was accomplished for the first time. In 1969, he returned to space as commander of the Apollo 11 mission and became the first man to walk on the Moon on July 20, 1969.

Yuri Gagarin
(1934–1968)

A Soviet cosmonaut, Gagarin was the first man to complete a space flight on April 12, 1961. On board the spacecraft Vostok 1, he made a revolution around the Earth during a flight that lasted 108 minutes. He died on March 27, 1968, in the crash of a military training flight.

Aleksei Leonov
(born 1934)

A Soviet cosmonaut, Leonov was the first man to complete a spacewalk on March 18, 1965, during the Voskhod 2 mission. His walk in a space suit lasted for twelve minutes, and he went as far as 15 feet (5 m) from the spacecraft. In July 1975, he returned to space on the U.S.-Soviet Apollo-Soyuz mission. He was later put in charge of the training of Soviet cosmonauts.

Index

Page numbers in italic indicate an illustration, and page numbers in bold indicate a definition on that page.